Success
for
Women

Success for

for

Women

Dare to Become
a Real Woman

Susan LaFlam

Published by Wordvision Publishers

ISBN 0-9707670-0-5

Printed in the United States of America

*This book is dedicated to my parents.
Thank you for your kindness and selfless
giving. You demonstrate love by always
thinking of others above yourselves.*

Table of Contents

Introduction

Picture a prospector searching high and low for gold. Finally, he finds a precious nugget. He quickly puts it in a small nugget bag and tucks it away in his shirt pocket nearest his heart. He cherishes the nugget because it means great wealth for him in the future.

This book contains many powerful "nuggets" specifically for women who desire to be successful. I hope that you will add some of my nuggets to your "nugget bag" and become richer along your success journey. Then share your riches with others as you have been enriched.

The Lord gave me a great desire and "burn" to share this empowering message with other women via this book. It is quite ironic that I wrote a book, since I used to *hate* to read. I was unaware that books can contain life-changing information. With a background in science and engineering, I was more comfortable with numbers than I was with words. But, my weaknesses and abilities did not limit God. It was clearly He who allowed me to complete this project.

Chapter 1
The Challenge

Are you tired of the mediocrity in your life? Are you frustrated that you aren't giving your best in your relationships? Do you feel defeated even before you begin each day? Do you know you are not living up to your potential?

Dare to do something so radical your life will never be the same... determine to be someone better than you are today. Dare to become a *real* woman, the beautiful, feminine person that God created you to be. You can improve in every area of your life. None of us has "arrived" yet. Accept the dare below daily. **Dare to succeed...**

Dare to take God at His Word.

Dare to believe with unwavering faith.

Dare to have hope in the future.

Dare to love unconditionally.

Dare to give sacrificially.

Dare to take a sincere interest in other people.

Dare to speak positively.

Dare to think the best of others.

Dare to build people up.

Dare to walk more confidently.

Dare to become stronger and healthier.

Dare to sleep peacefully.

Dare to smile radiantly.

Dare to look people in the eye.

Dare to let joy shine through your face.

Dare to think bigger.

Dare to dream bigger.

Dare to live bigger.

Read on and find out how.

Chapter 2
What Is Success?

Most people associate success with fame, fortune or some level of social status. Success is not an event or a list of achievements, but a *process*. If we define it on a moment by moment basis, **<u>success is simply the process of knowing the "right things" to do, knowing how to do them, having the courage to do them, and having the right character and attitude to handle the results.</u>** If this sounds like I define success as *being perfect all the time*, I am not. Let me clarify this definition further.

What do I mean by *knowing the "right things" to do*? I am talking about following God's plan for your life. He made you, right? He wants you to do what is right and succeed in each area of your life: your work, your marriage, your spiritual life, your health, your kids' lives, your finances, etc. Each day you are faced with many choices. Moment by moment, you can make the right decisions and follow God's best for your life. God's Word reveals His desires for you.

> *"For I want you always to see clearly the difference between right and wrong, and to be inwardly clean, no one being able to criticize you from now until our Lord returns. May you always be doing those good, kind things which show that you are a child of God, for this will bring much praise and glory to the Lord" (Philippians 1:10-11 (TLB)).*

How do you know *what the right things* are? As a Christian, you know God has a perfect will for your life. He has given His Holy Spirit and His Word to help guide you.

> *"The Lord is good and glad to teach the proper path to all who go astray; he will teach the ways that are right and best to those who humbly turn to him. And when we obey him, every path he guides us on is fragrant with his lovingkindness and his truth" (Psalm 25: 8-10 (TLB)).*

God gives you wonderful freedom to choose what you want to do. He has given you a mind that can dream and think creatively, a heart full of desires and a conscience to keep them all in check. He gives you the dreams, goals and desires deep within you.

If you are truly devoted to God and in tune with His plan, your desires will follow His desires for you. Obeying God's Word and daily communicating with Him can keep you on course with God's best for your life. This is what is "right" for you.

Will we always make the right decisions and choose what is best? Of course not; we are human and often choose to follow our flesh instead of the Spirit of God living within us. But with a repentant heart, we can adjust our direction and quickly get back on course. God is merciful and forgiving.

Gold Nugget:

God has given you a mind that can dream and think creatively, a heart full of desires and a conscience to keep them all in check.

What Do You Want to Do or Have or Become?

Many people breeze through life without knowing what they want or where they are going. But they are getting there fast and have lots of stress to prove it. That's like driving 65 mph down a highway with no destination in mind. You must choose a destination in life and plot your course, or you will wander aimlessly.

Take some time alone. Think the "sky is the limit" and "anything is possible" type thoughts. What dreams and goals has God given you? What do you truly want to do or have or become? Write *everything* you think of down in these three columns: "Do", "Have" and "Become".

Remember that no one will ever have to see your list of dreams and desires. Just let go and get started making your list. Once you begin, all kinds of dreams will flow from your mind. Maybe you want to lose 20 pounds or take a trip to Paris. You may want to have three personal disciples each year or have a pilot's license. Maybe you want to become an encouraging wife or become a counselor. Whatever you desires are, write them down. Some may sound silly, but you can sort them out later. Some may seem impossible.

I find this exercise difficult. It's hard to think big when we have had so many failures and disappointments. People may have even criticized you in the past for dreaming bigger or for wanting to improve your life.

Wait a day and carefully review your list. Evaluate if each item is realistic, attainable and specific enough? Pray over your list. Ask God to show you which things are important or urgent and which are not. Make sure your goals are morally right.

Knowing What Is "Right"

First evaluate what you want by what I call "basic moral values". These are non-negotiable guidelines that you abide by based on God's moral law. For example, it would be wrong for me to work for someone who wanted me to steal since I have a basic moral value that stealing is wrong (This one's in the Ten Commandments).

As believers our moral values should be based on God's Word. The Bible has black-and-white answers on many non-negotiable moral issues such as adultery. For example, I have decided that under no circumstance will I participate in infidelity because I want to obey God's standard of fidelity above my own flesh.

I once worked with a Christian man that refused to travel alone with a woman on business. He felt it was inappropriate for a married man to travel alone with another woman based on his moral values. He received much ridicule for his stance of moral integrity. I totally respected his courage to "do the right thing".

In addition to moral values, you must consider the impact of what you do on others. Will it help or hurt? Is it beneficial in the long run? Is it selfish? Is it wise? Is it legal, ethical and moral? What will the impact of what I do be in five, ten, twenty or fifty years?

> *"If any of you lacks wisdom, he should ask God, who gives generously to all without finding fault, and it will be given to him"* *(James 1:5).*

Pray about it. God wants to help us do what is right and pleasing to Him. Seek God and wait for His answers. The Holy Spirit and your God-given conscience will guide you to do what is right.

Moving from Goals to Action

Be realistic. You cannot begin working on every goal at once. This would be overwhelming, frustrating and foolish. Prioritize your list. What is the most critical thing you must start working on now? What goals will take a lifetime? Which goals are relatively easy that you can complete quickly? Remove any goals that are harmful or foolish.

Once you've decided what you want to work on, develop an *action plan* to achieve it. This may take some work. If a goal is worth achieving, it will be worth some effort in planning.

Get your plan streamlined into simple *action steps*. This may mean doing one or more small steps every day. Begin implementing your plan. You may need to keep a written log to help you record each action step you complete. It helps to document your progress or lack of it. Documentation can illuminate the truth between what we think we have done and what we actually have done.

For example, if your objective is to become an avid reader, you may set a goal of reading for at least 15 minutes every day. Select a great book that excites you, probably one recommended by someone you admire and respect. Make a chart on a bookmark and check each day that you read. After a month or so, you will probably have developed a habit of reading more than the fifteen minutes a day. Your habit may lead you to reading more than one book at a time!

In addition to having an action plan, you will need to *focus* on what you want to achieve or become. *Think about it* all you can. Picture yourself as you want to be.

Gold Nugget:

You will become what you think about.

Don't panic if you don't progress exactly according to your action plan. Your plan probably doesn't allow for any "curves" in the road. You will need to modify your action plan as needed along the way. Continuously improving your plan will get you to your goals quicker.

Knowing How to Do the Right Things

Success doesn't "just happen". That would be called *luck*. We must plan and prepare for success much like an athlete trains for a game. Have you ever heard of a middle-aged couch potato who decided he wanted to "walk on" and play for the New York Yankees?   Of course not. Athletes train for years for the opportunity to play Major League Baseball. Only those who have the required ability and determination will make it.

Have you ever heard of a minimum wage worker in his first week of work who was asked by the company's board of directors to become the new CEO just because he was a nice guy? That would be ludicrous. Just like a person would plan and prepare for years to become a CEO, so we must plan and prepare for our own success.

Successful people know they must grow and change. A seed cannot become a tree unless it ventures out of a comfortable shell by growing and stretching out into new fertile soil. The unknown can be uncomfortable and even scary at times. Sometimes we just have to step out in *faith*.

You may need to get some instruction, support or new skills to equip yourself for success. For instance, if you want to succeed in your marriage, you may need some new information to "reprogram your mind". It may be that what you know now isn't working very well. You may want to seek Christian counseling, associate with couples that have great marriages or start reading great books that will teach you how to have a great marriage.

Don't think you will get where you want to go by sitting where you are. Life is not a spectator sport; get off the bench. Be willing to change and improve to achieve your God-given potential.

Gold Nugget:

Successful people know
they must grow and change.

Having the Courage to Do the Right Things

It takes courage to do the right things. Knowing what is right and actually doing it are two different things. It is often a battle of the will. We must overcome our natural desire to do the acceptable, easy things in order to do the *right* and *best* things.

For example, a young mother resisted the temptation to buy new jewelry (on sale) for herself because she knew the money she had was designated in the monthly budget to buy food and clothing for her family. Even though buying the jewelry was not "wrong", she succeeded by exercising self-control and delaying gratification. Later, since she still wanted the jewelry, she planned and saved for it.   Because she waited, she enjoyed the jewelry much more (and guilt-free) than if she had purchased it with the household food budget.

Doing the right things requires a strong moral foundation, proper motivation and self-control.   As Christians, we can have self-control as a result of the Holy Spirit working in our lives.

> *"But the fruit of the Spirit is love, joy, peace, patience, kindness, goodness, faithfulness, gentleness and self-control (Galatians 5:22).*

Develop a *habit* of doing the right things daily.   Successful people have mastered this skill.   For example, we all know you can't become healthy in one week of crash dieting and working out in the gym.   Good health is simply obtained by *good habits* such as nutrition, exercise and rest.   No secrets here!

> *"We are what we repeatedly do. Excellence, then, is not an act, but a habit."*
>
> *- Aristotle*

I occasionally look at models on the covers of fitness magazines and think, "Wow, I wish I had a body like that." Then I remind myself, "If I did what she did, I might look more like she looks."   The cover model probably spends four hours a day working out in a gym, eats baked chicken (without skin) and never ever eats junk food.   She deserves to look so good! Her self-control and hard work give her the results she wants.

Gold Nugget:

**Doing the right things
requires a strong moral
foundation, proper
motivation and self-control.**

Character

In addition to personal integrity and moral values, your character should be humble. Humility is not thinking less of yourself, but having a proper view of yourself in relation to God and other people.

> *"Don't be selfish; don't live to make a good impression on others. Be humble, thinking of others as better than yourself" (Philippians 2:3(TLB)).*

Our personal achievements are only a result of the opportunities, abilities, dreams and desires God gives us. We must not become prideful and boast in our achievements and successes.

Gold Nugget:

**A successful person humbly
acknowledges that
everything is in God's
control and all good things
come from Him.**

Success also means admitting our failures. When we fail God or men, we should confess it, turn from it, make any necessary restitution and move on. This requires character and humility. Failing doesn't make us failures; it depends on how we respond to it and what we do next. A failure can either make us bitter or make us better. We can choose to improve and grow.

Gold Nugget:

**Failure is an event;
success is a process.**

Handling Adversity

Only a fool thinks his road to success will be smooth, free of potholes and slightly downhill. On the contrary, it will be rough, rocky and mostly uphill. But you know that anything worthwhile will not come without *adversity*.

Adversity can come in many different forms. It may be discouraging words from people who love you, failure after failure, tragedy, doubt or fear.

Part of this book was written while I was on vacation at the beach. While the rest of my family napped in the afternoon, I sat out on a sunny deck overlooking the ocean with my pen and notebook. As I assembled the outline for this chapter, a flock of seagulls hovered nearby looking for food. One of them peeked at my notebook to see what I was writing. He obviously didn't think much of it, as he dropped a "load of discouragement" right onto my open pages and me.

What did I do? I wiped it off and kept writing! It was a little gross, but mostly hilarious. Discouragement will be dropped on your journey to success, too. What will you do? *Just wipe it off and keep going!*

Don't forget to smile and laugh a little, too. Develop a sense of humor. Some of us need to relax and not be so serious all the time.

Don't let little things bother you so much. For instance, while driving or sitting in traffic, you can either let people *"get to you"* or you can *choose* to enjoy the ride. There are many ways you can use the time in your car wisely. You can have good conversation with your family, listen to good teaching or music or ... PRAY. (Who says you don't have time to pray?)

If you have children, remember they are watching you (even in the car). Children need to know grown-ups aren't always serious, uptight and frustrated when things don't go their way. Temper tantrums are for toddlers *not* adults. They need to see you exercise patience and a positive attitude.

Attitude

Along your success journey, you will have both good and bad experiences. How you react to them reflects your attitude. We have heard that *"attitude is everything"*. What kind of attitude should we have amidst seemingly "good" or "bad" situations?

"Your attitude should be the kind that was shown us by Jesus Christ, who, though he was God, did not demand and cling to his rights as God" (Philippians 2:5-6 (TLB)).

A young man went on a ski vacation with his friends. On the first day out on the slopes, he crashed into a tree and broke his leg. Not only was he in pain, but his vacation had come to a screeching halt. The situation appeared dismal and unfortunate. While he was in the hospital, he met a young nurse who eventually became his wife. Was his broken leg a bad experience or a *great one*? It all depends on *how* you look at it.

Gold Nugget:

It's not what happens that counts; it's how you handle it.

We will all have disappointments, failures and struggles. While we are in the midst of them, we may struggle to see any good in them. We may never understand their purpose. But, if you believe in a loving God, you can know that He always has His hand on you and is working all things for your good and His glory.

"And we know that in all things God works for the good of those who love him, who have been called according to his purpose" (Romans 8:28).

Qualities of Success

Successful people often have similar qualities. These qualities don't come easily. You are not born with them; they must be developed. They are developed by time and experience like friction polishes a rough gemstone to reveal its true beauty and value. Life's friction can help refine the qualities of success in us if we choose to allow it.

The following is a list of some of the qualities that *truly* successful people share:

Teachable

Successful people realize their need to learn. They know they don't "know it all". They take responsibility to invest in their own personal growth. They enjoy associating with people who are like what they want to become.

Humility

Successful people know that their physical, spiritual and mental abilities are gifts from God. They are willing to use them to serve others.

Hope

Successful people look forward to tomorrow with hope. They have hope for the future because they know *Who* holds it.

Self-Discipline

Successful people master their mind, body and emotions. They do what they ought to do, not just what they want to do.

Moral Integrity

Successful people know that they are accountable to God for what they say and do. (See 2 Corinthians 5:10.) They deal honestly and fairly with others. They obey their conscience even when it is difficult.

Positive

Successful people typically think positive thoughts and speak positive words about themselves and others. They know that negative thoughts and words are unproductive and harmful.

Ambition

Successful people are always seeking new opportunities for growth and service. They are not totally discontent (unhappy and whining) with where they are, but are always striving to improve and be their best.

Loving

Successful people are not self-centered, but loving. They are secure enough in themselves to truly extend their hands and love others.

Faith

Successful people rely on their faith. When others would doubt, they know that *"now faith is being sure of what we hope for and certain of what we do not see."* (Hebrews 11:1)

Chapter 3

Dare to Get Rid of the Waste in Your Life

Are you carrying around some extra baggage in your life? Do you want to lighten your load? In this chapter you will discover how to rid yourself of some of the waste in your life and *remain free* from it.

The Past Has Passed

> *"Now your attitudes and thoughts must all be constantly changing for the better. Yes, you must be a new and different person, holy and good. Clothe yourself with this new nature"* *(Ephesians 4:23-24 (TLB)).*

Are your attitudes changing for the better? Are you living like a new and different person? I love the imagery of clothing used in this verse. (God sure knows how to speak to women!) How do you feel when you take off your old, dirty work clothes, take a shower and put on a brand new dress for a dinner date? It's an amazing transformation. Like dirty work clothes, our old sinful nature is so ugly. But our new nature, the mind of Christ, is beautiful and new.

In 2 Corinthians 5:17 we read, *"Therefore if anyone is in Christ, he is a new creation; the old has gone, the new has come!"* My prayer is that you are a Christian and that you realize that you are a *new creation.*

Your past may contain some regretful situations or shameful habits. Don't let memories of your old sinful nature haunt you and steal your joy. No matter what your past has been, you need to *forget it.* Let go of it! When God saves us, He does it completely. He forgives our sins and takes away our guilt. Hallelujah!

As much as we would like to "undo" our past, we can't. We *can* make amends and restitution for our actions; we will talk about that later. We may even be living with some heavy consequences of our past. But our merciful God has allowed us to be conformed to his image regardless of our sinful past.

Gold Nugget:

You can become a new person with constantly improving thoughts, attitudes and actions.

A New Start

Don't you love the fresh newness of a brand new day? God sure knew what He was doing when He gave us relatively short days. Each day is like a new beginning. The cycle of the day gives us a fresh start every twenty-four hours.

Do you ever have days when you really blow it? Do you have days when you say hurtful words, break promises, let bad habits control you, carry around a rotten attitude, etc.? On these days we know we have failed to live as Christ-like ambassadors; our living was not excellent, or even average, but actually below mediocre. On days like these, I feel like slithering under a rock like a snake and emerging the next morning as the new creation that God intended.

God gives us a renewal process that is often referred to as "spiritual breathing", when we "exhale" (confess) our sin and "inhale" (be filled with the Holy Spirit). The same God who provided a wonderful redemptive plan also provided this maintenance program to keep our relationship with Him healthy. On a daily basis, we can be cleansed of the sin and guilt and renewed and empowered by His Spirit. This is powerful stuff!

We each face an internal struggle when our spirit wants to do what is right, but our flesh wants to do what is wrong. I remember as a child experiencing days where I seemed to continually disobey and act like a "grump". Since I had a moral conscience desiring to do right, this frustrated me. I wanted to "be good", but no matter how hard I tried, I just couldn't. Paul talks about his struggle with his flesh in

Romans 7:15, *"I do not understand what I do. For what I want to do I do not do, but what I hate I do."*

When my brother was a boy, he had an interesting remedy when he faced this internal battle: he had a process he called "nowing". In the midst of his displeasing behavior, he would stop, gain control of himself, fold his arms, and simply say "Now". This was his way of flushing the past and starting afresh with hopes of better behavior. What a great picture of renewal. After he became a Christian, he had the Holy Spirit's power when he would "now".

Gold Nugget:

**"Great is his faithfulness;
his lovingkindness begins
afresh each day."
(Lamentations 3:23 (TLB))**

Praise the God of new beginnings. We are new creatures in Christ.

Feel Like Running?

Do you ever feel like running? Running away from it all? If anyone ever felt like running, it was King David. Recall when he was convicted of his sin with Bathsheeba and follow-up murder of her husband Uriah. Nathan the prophet in 2 Samuel 12:14 told David of the Lord's judgement: David's son would die in seven days. It happened just as the

Lord spoke through Nathan.

After this string of tragedies, how would you have felt if you were David?   He was the chosen King of Israel and devoted to the Lord. He gave in to temptation, he wallowed in sin and guilt, and then his son died. David felt like running. But the story doesn't end like you think.

Immediately, when David found out his son was dead, he ran! **He ran to the Lord!** In 2 Samuel 12:19-20, we see *"...he (David) went into the house of the Lord and worshiped."* David didn't try to run away from it all. Instead, he ran to the Lord with whom he had an intimate relationship. David had truly repented and sought the Lord who chastised him. He was later blessed with another son named Solomon.

> *"By day the Lord directs his love, at night his song is with me- a prayer to the God of my life" (Psalm 42:8).*

So many times we want to run away from our problems. We think that if the problem would just go away, we could be happy and go on with life. There is no doubt that God can remove any problem, and sometimes He does. He wants us to seek Him in the midst of our struggles. We think we need fewer problems, but often it is more of God that we really need. Run to Him! His arms are open.

Gold Nugget:

When you feel like running, run to the Lord!

You Are Forgiven

Jesus provides the ultimate example of forgiveness. Absolutely sinless, Jesus was the perfect sacrifice to pay for our sins. Yet as He hung on the cross, Jesus spoke these words in Luke 23:34, *"Father, forgive them, for they do not know what they are doing."* Jesus taught men to forgive and demonstrated it with His life and death.

> *"For if you forgive men when they sin against you, your heavenly Father will also forgive you. But if you do not forgive men their sins, your Father will not forgive you"* (Matthew 6:14-15).

Peter once asked Jesus how many times a man should forgive another man who sins against him. Jesus replied in Matthew 18:22, *"I tell you, not seven times, but seventy-seven."* I think seven times sounds generous, or maybe even extreme, but Jesus said there should be no limit to our forgiveness toward others. There is no limit to God's forgiveness.

You Can Forgive

Harboring unforgiveness in our hearts can lead to bitterness. When we have been wronged, it is natural to become angry. God is never surprised by our emotions; remember that He made us. But, He also wrote the operating manual for our lives, *the Bible*.

In Exodus 34:6 we read that the Lord is "... *the compassionate and gracious God, slow to anger, abounding in love and faithfulness*." God's nature is love.

Gold Nugget:

God's nature is our basis
for forgiving others.

When someone wrongs us, we should get over it quickly, make amends and forgive completely. When we forgive, we give up the right to hold something against someone. Sounds like humility in action to me. Sounds like Jesus.

But, you say, "I have been hurt so badly and no one apologized to me." Forgive anyway. How? It's only possible because God forgave you. He set the ultimate example of forgiveness. The perfect sacrifice was made for our sins; Jesus' blood was enough to cover every sin we commit against God. His forgiveness is complete. Because God forgives, we should (and can) forgive.

In the days of the early church, Stephen was a man full of wisdom. He was empowered by the Holy Spirit as he spoke and performed miracles. His ministry convicted people of their sinful lives and empty religion. Many people began to angrily oppose Stephen, but he did not back down from the ministry God gave him. Eventually, his opposition stoned him. In Acts 7:60, we read that as they were stoning him he prayed, *"Lord, do not hold this sin against them."* Stephen had done no wrong and yet was killed for his faith. Yet by the power of the Holy Spirit, he was truly able to forgive his murderers.

Gold Nugget:

**When we forgive, we give
up the right to hold
something against someone.**

Forgive big. Relinquish your "right" to hold onto a wrong committed against you. That's what Jesus would do.

Crush Criticism

I greatly admire the Dale Carnegie training programs in human relations and effective speaking. Out of all the practical wisdom presented, one idea stuck with me more than any others: *"never criticize, condemn or complain"*. These bad habits are called *"the three C's"*. Eliminating "the three C's" from our speech (and thoughts) would improve every relationship we have.

Many people guard their speech around peers and co-workers, but let it all fly around their families. The people we love the most should receive our very best behavior and speech. Would you speak to your boss the way you speak to your husband? Would you speak to your friends the way you talk to your children? Would you be embarrassed if your pastor heard the conversation in your home?

Do you enjoy being around complainers and critics? How do they make you feel? No one likes to hear other people's gripes and complaints.

Have you ever asked someone, "How are you doing?"

Then you are afraid they are going to tell you how awful everything is. When you are around people like that, it's like getting sprayed by a skunk. The stink stays on you for a long time. As believers we must not let our tongues flap around without control.

Controlling the tongue requires submitting to the Spirit of God and letting Him rule our conversation. Our natural flesh is selfish, jealous and prideful; it produces critical, condemning, complaining speech. The Spirit of God is loving, thankful, joyful and kind; He produces this kind of conversation too. The battle is ongoing, and it is tough! You must daily choose the ways of God over your own sin nature.

> *"The words of a gossip are like choice morsels; they go down to a man's inmost parts" (Proverbs 18:8).*

What comes out of our mouths indicates what's in our hearts. It's hard to curse someone on the inside and praise him verbally. No matter what we say, people can usually tell what we are *really thinking*. We need to see other people as God sees them - precious and unique. We often think that we are more important or valuable to God than other people are. We should esteem others as better than ourselves.

I know of a lady, who not only doesn't criticize other people behind their backs, she doesn't criticize them in her mind. As a young girl, she began pretending that people could *read her mind*. She restrained herself from *even thinking* bad things about people. She used this little game to train herself not to think negative thoughts about other people. What a great way to eliminate negative thinking! Try it. Train your mind to reject negative thoughts. Discipline your mind as well as your mouth.

Vow to eliminate criticizing, condemning and complaining from your life. Replace these negative actions with positive ones.

Gold Nugget:

Replace *criticism* with appreciation. Replace *condemnation* with words that build others up. Replace *complaining* with thankfulness.

Worry

Do you worry about what people think or say about you? Do you constantly worry about how you look or what you have compared to others? Do you worry about the future and other things you can't control? In Matthew 6:27, Jesus said, *"Who of you by worrying can add a single hour to his life?"* When we worry about our needs and our future, we are focusing on ourselves as if those things are totally in our control. God wants us to be free from worry. Jesus gave us the answer in Matthew 6:33, *"But seek first his kingdom and his righteousness, and all these things will be given to you as well."* We must chose to focus on Him, seek Him and trust Him to meet our needs.

Forget Fear

I have had many women tell me that their thoughts are dominated by *fear*. This may include fear of danger, fear of harm, fear for their family's safety or fear of losing someone precious. Letting these types of fearful thoughts control your mind puts you in bondage.

Fear can close up your soul so tight that you can't give or receive love, you can't grow or help other people grow, and you can't live up to your God-given potential. It's like wearing a shoe three sizes too small - the results are painful, not pretty. Fear can cripple and destroy.

Didn't Jesus come to set us free from this type of stuff? The opposite of fear is faith in a God who is in control of *everything*. We know this is true, but so many are in the habit of letting fear control their lives. When we dwell in fear, we forget *Whose* children we are. It is our human nature to fear, but it's not God's nature. God is love.

Most everything we fear will *never* happen. And even if it does, can't we trust God to take care of us? Nothing we fear is too big for mighty God to handle. I like the Psalmist's confidence in God in Psalms 46:2 where he writes, *"Therefore we will not fear, though the earth give way and the mountains fall into the heart of the sea."*

When I first married, I was overwhelmed with fear of losing my husband in an accident. A few weeks after our wedding, he went to Europe on business. I struggled with giant waves of fear. When I felt myself drowning, I dove headfirst into the Word of God to find answers. That week I settled that issue. The Lord gave me a wonderful gift in my husband, and He could choose to take him away. If so, I determined in my heart that I would go on and trust His sovereign plan. It's funny how I seldom have this fear anymore. Whatever your greatest fear, face it and seek the Lord about it. Don't let go until it is settled. He *delights* in our calls for help.

We are human and will have fearful thoughts. What's important is *what* we do with those thoughts. Confront them. Ask yourself, "Is this fear real? Does God's Word address this particular thought in the Bible?" Force these fearful thoughts through the filter of God's Word. Then wrap them up with faith and throw them away. Replace fearful thoughts with God's Word and dwell on His character.

In 2 Corinthians 7:5-6, the Apostle Paul describes one of the times in his ministry where he was *"harassed at every turn - conflicts on the outside, fears within."* It is comforting to know that even a spiritual giant like Paul admits his fear. He then acknowledges, *"But God, who comforts the downcast, comforted us by the coming of Titus."* We too can ask God for comfort amidst our fears. He is our Comforter.

Faith in the Fiery Furnace

Speaking of fear, remember young Shadrach, Meshach and Abednego (the Jewish boys taken captive to be trained as Babylonian leaders)? They obeyed God's command not to worship any other gods and, in doing so, disobeyed the King. When threatened with the doom of death in a blazing furnace, how did they respond? See Daniel 3:16-18.

Did they have fear when they saw the fiery furnace? I would guess they weren't too excited about it! But we do know they were men of faith. They laughed in the face of fear because they trusted totally in their God who was able to deliver them. Even if He didn't deliver them, they would remain faithful. Wow, can you trust your God like that? You have the same God that they did, and He hasn't changed over the years.

Purge the "Junk" in Your Life

I'm not just talking about cleaning out all the clothes in your closet that you haven't worn for five years. We've just talked about getting rid of fear, sin, unforgiveness, worry and a critical spirit. Now I want to discuss getting rid of some other "junk", *time-wasters* and *worthless activities* that weigh your life down. This junk can keep you from doing the really *important* things and accomplishing the truly **great** things you are called to do.

Let's look at a few of the potential "junk" piles.

1. The PHONE!!!

Do you waste time on the phone? How many times do people call you just to chat (or maybe gossip)? Before you know it, you have talked for forty-five minutes about *nothing*. If you get a call that you sense is not urgent, and you really don't have time to chat, simply say, "I can't talk now. Should I call you later?" The caller will probably state her business in ten seconds and tell you there's no need to call back.

2. Activities

We are a generation of active, busy people. We feel "successful" when we are involved in lots of activities with lots of other busy people. We are defined by what we do, so we need to make sure we are doing not just good things, but the very best things. Most of our activities are not bad things; they are probably good for us. However, we need to make sure they are in line with our priorities. For example, playing on three softball teams is great for your fitness and social life, but it may conflict with the higher priority of raising your family. Sometimes, we should say "No" to good things.

A very wealthy man was once criticized by some members of his church because he did not volunteer to help repaint the church interior. None of them knew how very generous he had always been with the tremendous wealth with which the Lord had blessed him. His time was his greatest resource. Instead of spending one day painting at the church, he could earn enough money to have ten churches painted. He gave up something good for what was best.

Families can be dominated by children's activities. These things are great and can be so valuable in developing our children. But before allowing your child to participate in an activity, ask yourself "why" you and your child should be involved in it and "what" it will require of both your child and your entire family. After careful thought you may find that some children's activities provide nothing good for your child besides busyness, stress and reheated dinners. Remember *you*, not your child, are the parent, and you must decide what is best for your family. Follow your conscience.

3. Television and Entertainment

Do you find yourself uncomfortable without the television on? Could you do without it for a week? Try it. You will be surprised to find more hours in the day and new opportunities to communicate with your family.

Are you addicted to movies? I've never understood why some people "have" to go see every movie that Hollywood produces, just because it is released in theatres. Be cautious about the content of movies. Guard what goes into your mind and heart.

Here's a new idea - read a book. How many books have you read lately? I don't mean Dr. Suess. Read something positive that will inspire you, educate you, encourage you and push you toward your dreams and goals.

I can hear you saying, "But I'm just not a reader." You can become one! I never liked reading because I read very slowly and resented being forced to read meaningless books in school. But as an adult, I have become an avid reader. I have improved my life by reading good books. You can too!

4. Idle Conversation

I define idle conversation as talking about nothing

beneficial to either party. When you are at work, do you waste time talking about a mediocre television show you saw the night before or about a traffic jam on the way to work? Who cares? Use your words to talk about something worthwhile. Avoid being trapped in conversation with people who are always negative, critical or whining. (If you happen to be trapped next to one on an airplane, make sure you have a good book to read.)

What should we talk about? In Colossians 4:6 (TLB), we find out: *"Let your conversation be gracious as well as sensible, for then you will have the right answer for everyone."* Our words should be sensible and wholesome. The spoken word is powerful for building up others and communicating the love of the Lord in our lives. As Christians, our conversation should be different from that of the world.

Have you thought about some of the "junk" you need to purge from your life? Do you have some time-wasters and worthless activities? I'm not saying we should drop everything and sit around doing nothing. That would be slothful.

The more I observe successful people, the more I realize that they are *very busy people* doing the things they are passionate about. They have learned how to be disciplined and efficient, doing the *important* and *productive* things. They do not waste time doing the mundane things that waste their time, energy and resources. Doing the *right things* can actually energize you.

*"Either you run the day, or the day runs
you."*

- Jim Rohn

Prioritize the Important "Stuff"

What's really important to you?   Have you listed your
priorities? Are they truly in this order?

Priority 1: God

Priority 2: Husband

Priority 3: Children

Priority 4: Ministry

Priority 5: Work

Priority 6: Everything else

The first five priorities in this list can (and should) take
most of your time. This leaves little time for Priority 6, the
"everything else" that fills our lives. There may be a hundred
things included in Priority 6 that can quickly creep to the top
of the list. Watch out!

Most women struggle to maintain their top two priorities
as God and husband.   Priorities 3-6 seem to scream,
"URGENT!" and take our focus from God and our marriage
relationship. We must fight to keep them on top.

Get Organized

Here it comes, ladies. It's time to organize. Let me first
tell you this is quite a struggle for me. If you are like myself

and do not have a personality that thrives on organization, you will be tempted to skip this part. If you are the type who arranges your pantry in alphabetical order, you are probably eager to read this section.

Gold Nugget:

Disorganization drains your time, your energy and your resources like a hole in a bathtub.

Believe it or not, some personality types can function with stuff in random piles everywhere. We just know which stuff is in which pile. Some of you cringe at the thought of having "stuff in piles". Where do you fall on the organization spectrum? Perhaps somewhere in the middle?

I've operated in both extreme organization and utter randomness. I'm convinced that organization is better than chaos. We were created in God's image. The Bible reveals to us a God of order who plans and leaves nothing to randomness. In Genesis 1:2, we read, *"Now the earth was at first a shapeless, chaotic mass, with the Spirit of God brooding over the dark vapors."* In only six days God transformed this formless planet into an awesome showcase of His glory. With every "Let there be" command spoken, He revealed another spectacular display of His power. Nothing was by chance. Can you imagine if during the awesome Creation week, God misplaced the moon behind the sun? Not for a second has the moon ever been a millimeter out of the path God planned for it.

We all know how to organize, but many of us are just too lazy to start. We think that since we've never been organized, "Why bother starting now?" or "Even if I start, it will be impossible to maintain any type of a system." We would all be surprised how fun a little organization can be, how freeing it can be, and how much time it can save us in the long run.

It's Piled Up to the Ceiling, So Where Do I Begin?

1. Start small.

For some, it may be your lingerie drawer or the shoes on the floor in your closet. For others, it may be the pantry or the whole kitchen. How about the garage or the attic? What area could you get the most bang for your buck? Little successes breed big successes.

Pull out everything and designate it either as "garbage", "give away", "can't decide right now" or "definitely keep". Once you have these piles, you can then work with each one without feeling overwhelmed. Process these piles until everything is in its place. Then keep it there.

2. Develop a system.

A system is having a place for everything. A system only works when everyone involved knows where things go and they are *capable* and *responsible* for maintaining the system. Perhaps your children and husband would keep things more orderly if they understood the system and knew what was expected of them. Be patient, very patient; they may not share your same enthusiasm for organization.

When working as an engineer, I witnessed a manufacturing company incorporate a system where every part, tool and piece of equipment was assigned a logical place via a label or outline. For example, on a board where tools were hung, outlines were drawn around the tools to indicate their storage places. A mechanic would then know to put the wrench on the wrench-shaped outline. This was a huge time saver. Each mechanic then knew where each tool could be found and could tell at a glance which ones were missing. No more time was wasted fumbling around in drawers and toolboxes looking for a particular tool. This example sounds extreme, but the principles apply to where and how we store things at home or work. Think about what improvements you could make in your system with a few labels.

3. <u>Write it down.</u>

I am a list-maker (although rarely for groceries). I make lists on envelopes, post-it notes, napkins and just about anything. I like to keep short, quick "to-do" lists that I can quickly complete and throw away. Lists do not make me an organized person (just ask my husband), but they are great tools to help me focus on the tasks at hand.

Do you use a daily or monthly planner? I've never

meet a person who properly used one that complained it didn't save them time and make them more efficient.

Make daily "to-do" lists and separate "to-call" lists. This is so simple, yet so powerful! What you don't get done on today's list, just transfer to the next day if it is still worth doing. When you make your "to do" list, do the *most dreaded* task first. After that you won't be so inclined to procrastinate. And, best of all, you'll feel great for doing it.

Gold Nugget:

Eliminate the unnecessary; it only drains your energy.

Start today getting rid of the junk and time-wasters in your life. Live free of clutter. You will have more room and time for the important things that really matter.

Chapter 4

Dare to Build the Inner You

In this chapter we will look at some principles that will:

- Build a solid foundation for your life
- Give you proper self-esteem
- Give you a basis for improving your life

Look Inside to See if You're a Winner

Do you ever buy a bag, box or bottle with these words on the package: "Look inside to see if you're a winner"? You rush home from the grocery positive that you've won the one million-dollar prize or the dream home. You think you might at least have won a Hawaiian vacation or a new CD player. You rip open the package to find the words "Sorry, try again". It might as well say "LOSER!"

Depending on your self-image that day, it can either roll

off your back or stick like peanut butter in the roof of your mouth. Be assured that your being a winner is NOT determined by what's written inside a bag of potato chips.

But there is *some* truth to the statement: "Look inside to see if you're a winner." What really matters is your inside relationship with your Creator that begins with faith in Christ. It is His endowment of your unique abilities and gifts and what you do with them. It's also your attitude. It is *what's inside you* that makes you a winner.

You may not have the face of a cover girl, the figure of a model or the brains of a CEO, but you are still a winner if you are in sync with God's plan for your life. You win when you accomplish the things He wants you to do.

It's all in *Who* you know! *I know* that I know Jesus Christ as my Savior and have accepted His plan for eternity. Yes, the winners will be in heaven. I hope to see you there!

Who Are You, Anyway?

If you are a Christian, you should know who you are because of *Whose* you are. You are a child of the King. You can be confident not only in God's perfect redemptive plan, but also in the blessings of the redeemed. Here are a few of the promises found in God's Word about you:

- You are loved. (Romans 5:8)

- You are redeemed and forgiven. (Ephesians 1:7)

- You are saved completely. (Hebrews 7:25)

- You possess eternal life. (John 3:36)

- You are an adopted child of God. (Romans 8:15-17)

- You are indwelt by the Holy Spirit. (I Corinthians 3:16)

- You are free from the controlling power of sin. (Romans 8:2)

- You have hope. (Hebrews 6:19)

What credentials we have as servants of Christ! There are many more promises to believers in the Scriptures. Read these promises whenever you start to doubt your worth. Thank God for making you worthy.

What Are You Worth?

Did you ever wonder if you were kidnapped what the ransom amount would be? And, more importantly, would anyone really be willing to pay it for you? Be assured; you were bought with the highest price. With His very life, Jesus paid the price to cover your sins and give you eternal life with Him. The *payment* established your *value*. You are extremely valuable to God.

I must confess that I fail to see myself as the valuable treasure that God so willingly redeemed to Himself with His Son's life. My self-worth is so heavily influenced by the opinions of others and by my failures and shortcomings. I need to stand on what God says about me, not what I feel or what others think. The Word of God is loaded with these truths.

If you struggle with your self-worth, memorize and claim the following verse:

> *"So now, since we have been made right in God's sight by faith in his promises, we can have real peace with him because of what Jesus Christ our Lord has done for us. For because of our faith, he has brought us into this place of highest privilege where we now stand, and we confidently and joyfully look forward to actually becoming all that God has in mind for us to be" (Romans 5:1,2 (TLB)).*

Do you ever wonder if people would like you if they really knew the *real* you? You see, God *really* knows you (*because He made you*), and He *still* loves you. You are truly valuable. It is awesome that each of us is worth that much to God.

> *"O Lord, you have examined my heart and know everything about me" (Psalm 139:1 (TLB)).*

It's O.K. to like yourself without being self-centered or egotistical. A healthy self-image is not to be confused with vanity or pride. It is God alone who gives us our worth. A healthy sense of self-worth frees us to acknowledge the greatness of God and the value of people. It is never too late to develop a healthy self-image.

Gold Nugget:

When we have a proper self-worth, we are free to love others and see them as God does. We can stop worrying about ourselves and focus on the needs of others.

Never Alone

> *"How precious it is, Lord, to realize that you are thinking about me constantly! I can't even count how many times a day your thoughts turn toward me. And when I waken in the morning, you are still thinking of me!" (Psalm 139:17,18 (TLB)).*

It blows my mind to think that God is thinking of me when I wake up in the morning. All I'm thinking about is turning on the coffeepot. Even in my grogginess He already knows what I dreamed about, how I feel, what I'm going to do that day and whom I will meet. We should greet Him early in the day. He's already up, ready to talk.

We all feel lonely at times. Even among a group of people we can still feel lonely. It's all about *relationships*. If we are with people with whom we have no relationship, we can feel totally alone. But if we have a personal relationship with God, we have the Holy Spirit with us all the time. God's throne is accessible via prayer 24 hours a day - and you'll never get a busy signal!

There is never a moment when God says, "Oops! I lost track of Susan LaFlam for a few hours. I wonder if she is O.K.?" God never loses track of us, but we *can* lose track of Him. How many hours, days or weeks do we go without focusing on God and nourishing our relationship with Him?

When I was in college, I often didn't have dates on the weekend. Sometimes I would have "dates" with God. These were special times of worship and prayer. I spent a few hours alone in my bedroom reading God's Word and singing (loudly since everyone else was out). I had a blast! We had a sweet fellowship and grew so much closer. These were some precious times with God that I'll never forget. As my life progressed (frankly, I got older), it has been harder to find those precious times alone with God. There seem to be so many more interruptions now. But He always meets with me when I break away and give Him my full attention. Thank you, Abba, Father, for remaining true and faithful every moment of my life.

Gold Nugget:

**Be aware of His daily
presence in your life.
Moment by moment, He is
all you need.**

We Don't Have to Understand

Every night people cry themselves to sleep asking God,

"Why?" Hurting people ask God why there is suffering, pain, death, sorrow and injustice in this world. Why do people die even though we pray for their healing? Why are others innocent victims of tragedy?

Along with our human nature, come the results of sin: sickness, pain, sorrow and death. We deserve all these things because we are members of the sinful human race. God in his mercy has also allowed us to have the gifts of eternal life, health, love, joy and peace. We should have grateful hearts because we don't deserve any of these wonderful blessings.

We don't always have to understand, but it's O.K. to ask, "Why, God?" God made us in His image with the ability to think, wonder, reason and feel emotions. God is never surprised or angry when we ask "why?" In fact, He is glad when we seek Him. He is the 24-hour a day infinite source of love, power and wisdom. He never tires of our calls for help.

God wants us to seek Him for answers. Sometimes the answer is just for us to trust Him. That is heavy-duty, industrial strength faith. When we don't understand, we must cling to the very nature of God - LOVE.

Gold Nugget:

One thing we know about God's loving character is that He never makes a mistake. Nothing is out of His control.

Who's Holding the Rope?

When working as an engineer, one of my job responsibilities was to perform occasional safety inspections. One day I had to crawl into an enormous boiler vessel and physically inspect it to ensure it was safe for mechanics to perform some maintenance activities. Before you enter such a closed vessel, you must make sure that there is a way that someone can quickly get you out if there is a problem inside, such as a deadly gas leak. The safety gear consists of leather straps buckled around your ankles attached to long ropes. Someone outside the vessel holds the other ends of the ropes. The ropes become your potential lifelines to safety if you needed to be quickly removed from the vessel.

As you can imagine, I was a little nervous about this dirty and potentially risky situation. But I had a real peace when I knew *who* would be holding the ropes: a man called "Big Jim". That was his real name, Big Jim. He was probably the largest man I have ever met, at least seven feet tall and equally as burly. Each of his hands was bigger than my hardhat. Big Jim was a contractor with whom I had worked for a while. He had always been so kind and helpful to me. He put me at ease when he said, "Miss Susan, don't you worry. If anything happens, I'll get you out." And I knew he meant it. I knew I would be safe if Big Jim was holding the ropes. I totally trusted in him and his ability to save me.

When it comes to the challenging situations of life, do we know *Who* is holding the ropes? He's mightier than Big Jim: He is our Father God. He will never let us go. He's the Great Shepherd protecting and caring for us. He's always faithful, loving and kind.

God promised to never leave us. When Moses assured Joshua of God's continued protection and deliverance in Deuteronomy 31:6, he said, *"Be strong and courageous. Do not be afraid or terrified because of them, for the Lord your God goes with you; he will never leave you nor forsake you."* It was as if Moses told Joshua, "Don't worry! Remember the Lord your God has the ropes." He provides the faith when we have fear. He supplies the peace when we worry.

So relax. Look back and see Who is holding your ropes. Thank you, Jesus, I'm safe.

Ask for Wisdom

> *"If any of you lacks wisdom, he should ask God, who gives generously to all without finding fault, and it will be given to him"* *(James 1:5).*

I often pray aloud in the car with my children, particularly at the beginning of the day. One day I asked my four-year-old son if there was anything specific that he wanted to pray about. He said, "Yes, Mommy, I want to ask God to give me wisdom to make me a wise son." What a precious request. As the tears streaked down my cheeks, I prayed for his request.

I have no doubt that God is giving wisdom to my son. It is evident. God promised it. If I promised to give my child breakfast when he woke up in the morning, would I do it? Of course I would. How much more does our Father give us what He promises? Claim James 1:5 as your prayer. We can always take God at his word.

I also prayed, "Thank you, God, for reminding me to *ask for wisdom*." How did a four-year-old know to ask God for wisdom? He has unwavering faith in a mighty God. His God truly is all-powerful. His God is the God that gave wisdom and faith to his Bible heroes, David, Daniel and Joseph. My son reads the Bible stories about these men of faith and learns just how big God is. He believes in this same God with all his childish heart. I pray, "God, give me that childlike faith."

Feed Your Brain Daily

You are what you eat. Of course, we have heard this for years from the health experts. (Maybe I should put down my cookie as I write this section.) I am not referring to merely physical food that we eat. Let's discuss mental food - what we feed our brains.

Mental food is the stuff we put in our minds through reading, watching and hearing. The books, magazines, newspapers, television, movies, music and conversation that we hear are like *food for our minds*. All this "mental food" goes into our giant computer-like brains where it is stored.

The images and information we ingest help form our belief systems and attitudes. I know people who watch the evening news every night before bed and wonder why they arise fearful and with a negative, hopeless outlook on life. I am not at all surprised! What we put into our minds is what we believe and think about.

I remember as a teenager trying to justify inappropriate music or television shows to my parents by claiming, "It won't hurt me. I can handle it." Wrong! If you know something is not good for you, obey your conscience and just don't let it into your mind. You can't erase the impression it leaves in your mind.

Consuming inappropriate "mental food" can be more harmful than a junk food diet. Some of the evils and tragedies in our society are rooted in bad mental diets. Consider violence, cynicism, disrespect for authority and pornography.

Examine yourself. Are you a "mental junk-food junky"? You can't do anything about the past, but you can change the future. Make a decision to exercise self-control in your life. Guard your mind. Change your mental diet.

Run from negative input. It is all around you, but you can avoid some of it. If what you watch on television is negative input, turn it off. If your friends are a source of negative input, find some new friends. It is worth making some changes in your life to nourish yourself with wholesome "mental food".

Gold Nugget:

Consuming inappropriate "mental food" can be more harmful than a junk food diet.

Let's look at some of the benefits of a strict mental diet. If you discipline yourself to a positive, wholesome mental diet, people will notice a "different you". The benefits are life-changing. Here are a few of the benefits you will experience:

- You will have a more optimistic view of life.

- You will be more pleasant to be around.

- You will be more enthusiastic.

- You will have more hope.

- You will believe in yourself and others.

- You will worry less and sleep more peacefully.

- You will be more productive.

What Goes In... Comes Out

A family came to visit with their two small children. As they were politely removing their coats inside the front door, one of the preschoolers was having trouble. As he struggled with his zipper, he blurted out a shocking string of profanity. It was quite an embarrassing moment for all. The parents shamefully admitted that he learned it from them. *What goes in... comes out.*

The words we speak to our children are like dollars deposited in a bank. Eventually we will make a withdrawal and get what we put in plus accumulated interest. It's not surprising that children who are told they won't amount to anything *usually don't*. And those that are encouraged to do great things *often do*.

Gold Nugget:

You can and must choose what you put into your mind. It will determine your thoughts, your actions and your speech.

In addition to the conversation we hear, music, television, magazines and books are also significant inputs in our lives: good or bad. Do the things we allow into our lives promote irreverence, violence, promiscuity, disrespect for authority, irresponsibility and mediocrity? If so, we must change our inputs. These are not the things we want coming out of our minds and mouths, so why put them in at all? You can and **must choose** what you put into your mind. The things that occupy your mind will determine your thoughts, your actions and your speech.

Consider the people with whom you associate. What do they allow to occupy their minds? Would you like your children to grow up to be like them? Would you like to have their values and character? I hope so, because if you continue to hang around them, your values will become like theirs, good or bad. You will talk like them and act like them. Evaluate your close relationships. You may need to find some new friends.

Filter what goes into your mind by your value system. It is O.K. if you refuse to see a movie because it promotes immorality. I think Jesus would if He were on earth today. Take a hard look at what you are reading and listening to. Can you find something better that will improve you and your character? The choice is yours.

If you filter out all the bad stuff, what should you put into your mind? We find the answer in Philippians 4:8 (TLB) *"...Fix your thoughts on what is true and good and right. Think about things that are pure and lovely, and dwell on the fine, good things in others. Think about all you can praise God for and be glad about."* If we put these good things in, they will eventually come out.

What you put into your mind will impact your character, values and your future. Choose your mental food wisely.

Abolish Negative Thinking

Here's a familiar scenario. You see someone in a store that you know from somewhere, but you don't remember his or her name. You know you should say "Hello" and introduce yourself with, "Hi, I think I know you." But immediately your mind assumes the *negative* outcome, "They don't know me and don't really care to. Besides, they look like they are in a hurry." So you agree with your mind and do the only logical thing, walk the other way pretending you don't see them. Sound familiar? Does giving in to this kind of negative thinking make you feel weak and insecure?

Negative thinking is **destructive**. It dooms you to failure before you try. Stop thinking the worst will happen. We don't live under "Murphy's law"; we abide by God's law.

A lady was interviewing for a job with a company with which she really wanted to work. Before the interview she thought, "I'll give it my best, but I'll probably never hear from them again." She might as well have skipped the interview. With those negative thoughts running through her mind, she would not have come across as a good potential employee. She doomed herself with her negative self-talk. We are all guilty of it. On the other hand, if she had positive thoughts about how qualified she was for the job, she would have appeared more capable and desirable to the company.

I am not against *realistic* thinking. For example, if you are 6'2" tall and weight 250 pounds, you will probably not be a successful jockey, no matter how positively you think about it. Be realistic. The facts are the facts, but *sometimes* the facts can be overcome.

We have seen through history many men and women who did the seemingly impossible because they **would not succumb** to negative thinking. Do you know how many successive failures at business and politics Abraham Lincoln experienced before he became President of the United States? Plenty! Negative self-talk would tell him, "Quit trying, you will never succeed." Instead, he listened to that small voice in his heart, which said, "You must keep trying, Abe, and you **will succeed**."

A young lady struggled with being overweight most of her life. To compensate for her low self-esteem, she became loud and obnoxious to draw attention to herself and *make* people like her. She'd tried desperately to lose weight, but always gave in to her negative thoughts, "Why bother, you'll always be fat". Finally, she kicked those negative thoughts out of her head and replaced them with visions of who she wanted to become. These visions motivated her to work hard. She began to believe she could change. Eventually, the pounds started coming off. The biggest change was on the inside; she became an others-focused person with a gentle spirit. To this day she has never given in to her old "stinking thinking" that held her in bondage for years.

Chapter 5
Dare to Build the Outer You

Your Health

I don't need to say much about this topic since we are probably the most "health-educated" generation to ever live. Even our children learn about fat grams and the food groups in preschool. We know the basics of exercise, nutrition, rest, avoiding toxic substances, etc. We all know the right way to take care of our bodies to help them live long and healthy, but it is obvious that we don't all do it. This is sad and sobering.

Here are some reasons why a person doesn't work to be healthy:

1. She doesn't value herself. Her self-esteem is so low that she doesn't feel worthy of maintaining her body or improving her health.

2. She is *lazy*. She knows what she should be doing, but she just doesn't do it. Her health is a low priority.

Excuses are plentiful; motivation is scarce.

3. She is addicted to an unhealthy lifestyle and doesn't know how to be free. She needs to know God's power can overcome and set her free from whatever holds her captive. She must envision her life how she wants it to be and develop a plan to get there. She may need to seek professional help or counseling.

Your Appearance

Do you think your outer appearance is important? Are you comfortable with how you look and how you dress? Are you the best you can be when it comes to your appearance? Do you fuss and worry about your appearance constantly?

Many of us fall into extremes when it comes to our appearance. On one extreme, some are obsessed with it. While on the other extreme, some may not put any time or effort toward their outer appearance. There is a balance. You must know what is the right amount of emphasis for you.

There is no question that our inner beauty, that of a gentle spirit, is far more important than our outer appearance. But a person's outward appearance is seen long before her fine character is revealed. First impressions are made within 10 seconds of meeting someone on the basis of appearance, body language and conversation. When someone first meets you, what do they think of you and your appearance? Would they guess you are a Christian? Do they think you care about your appearance and body (the temple of God)?

"Don't you know that you yourselves are God's temple and that God's Spirit lives in you?" (I Corinthians 3:16).

God gave us each the body we have; that's all we have to work with. It's easy to compare ourselves with others and envy someone else's face or figure. We must accept what God has given us and make the best of it. These bodies are only temporary homes, anyway. Man sees the outside, but God sees the heart inside.

We should spend more time developing our inner beauty than our outward physical beauty. In her book, *Disciplines of the Beautiful Woman* (Word, Inc.), Anne Ortlund points out that in Proverbs 31, only one verse out of twenty-two speaks about the wise woman's appearance while the other twenty-one verses describe her character. She prays, *"Father, I want to give 1/22 of my time to making myself as outwardly beautiful as I can; and I want to give all the rest of my time, 21/22 of my life, to becoming wise, kind, godly, hardworking, and the rest."* That puts it into perspective.

It is important to look our best as much as possible. I remember those early days of motherhood when I often greeted my husband at the end of the day without ever changing out of my nightgown, taking a shower, glancing at my hair in the mirror or applying any makeup. (I had brushed my teeth.) What a lovely sight I must have been! My husband deserved much better than this. I am his chosen bride, the one for whom he forsakes all others. I don't want him to forget it.

Do you want your husband to be delighted with your

appearance? It takes some effort to maintain yourself, but it's worth it. Do not neglect yourself. Spend a minimal amount of time everyday on your appearance.

Your Hair and Nails

Your hair should be neat and flattering (the way your husband likes it). It doesn't hurt to update your hairstyle every few years - you will look YOUNGER if you follow the trends. Nails are often overlooked. They should be neatly groomed and never bitten.

Your Face

I believe in skin care and make-up. The old saying "A fresh coat of paint makes any old barn look better" is true. A little make-up can do wonders for all of us. More make-up is not necessarily better. Learn how the experts apply make-up and use it to flatter your best features and minimize your imperfections. The art of make-up takes practice and a little education.

Your Clothes

> *"Not every woman in old slippers can manage to look like Cinderella."*
>
> *- Don Marquis*

Pay attention to fashion *trends*, NOT fads. Trends will be around for several years, but fads will probably only last for one season.

Buy the best you can afford. A few quality outfits can go a long way. You don't necessarily have to spend a fortune on clothes to look great, but you do need to shop wisely and purchase items that fit your image, flatter you and fit your body properly. I know women that spend a great deal of money on their clothes every year and still don't look well dressed.

Make mental notes when you get compliments on your clothing (both colors and styles). Outside opinions are much more objective than our own. Your clothes should compliment you and **create the impression** you want to give. They should never be shocking or inappropriate for the occasion.

We often make assumptions about a person's values and personality simply by observing their outer appearance. Your true (inner) person *is reflected* in your outer appearance, by the way you dress and groom yourself.

The opposite is also true: your outward appearance can impact your inner feelings. My favorite song from the musical *Hello, Dolly* is *"Put on your Sunday clothes when you feel down and out."* Have you noticed how you perk up when you put on your finest clothes? You seem to walk with more confidence and exude a better attitude.

Caution: we should not be prideful by dressing to impress or attract attention. *Your outer appearance should reflect the character-building work God is doing on the inside.*

Gold Nugget:

Make the most of your appearance. It *reflects* who your are on the *inside*.

The Ultimate Facelift

I don't know a woman alive that doesn't want to look more beautiful; that's just how God made us. But let's face it, God also made gravity.

The ultimate facelift does not require surgery or expensive creams. It's instantaneous, absolutely free and available to everyone. It's a SMILE! That's right, you can dramatically improve the appearance of your face by smiling. Nothing is more captivating than the cheerfulness of a woman. It's very feminine.

A radiant smile speaks of cheerfulness in the heart. It casts its radiance upon all who see it. When you give a smile, you almost demand one back. Who wouldn't rather see a joyous smile than a dreary frown?

> *"A happy heart makes the face cheerful,*
> *but heartache crushes the spirit" (Proverbs*
> *15:13).*

Practice Smiling

Do you ever walk by a mirror and catch a glimpse of yourself only to be shocked by your grumpy countenance? I sure have; it's a scary sight. We must *practice* smiling.

Train the muscles in your face to smile like you would train your hands to play the piano. Make a conscious effort to do it, and it will soon become natural. Place a small mirror near your telephone so you can remind yourself to smile while talking on the phone. It's amazing how much more pleasant your voice is when you are smiling.

> *"A cheerful look brings joy to the heart,*
> *and good news gives health to the bones"*
> *(Proverbs 15:30).*

Practice smiling. I guarantee you will feel better, and so will those around you. But here's a warning; it might just be contagious!

Chapter 6
Dare to Improve Your Behavior

The Magnificent Proverbs 31 Woman

I love the passage found in Proverbs 31:10-31 that describes this magnificent wise woman. We, as Christian women, wish deep down that this description could be written about our own lives. The woman described in this passage is one who does it all, has it all and probably does it with great finesse. She may be the envy of her neighborhood or church. She is a benchmark for all of us.

Many wonderful Bible studies are available on this passage. I do highly recommend them for personal or group study. So much has already been written about this passage (Proverbs 31) that I only want to devote a small section of this book to it.

There are a few character traits that really jump out at me about the magnificent Proverbs 31 woman:

1. She is not lazy.

Her daily tasks are not dependent on the television schedule, how she feels or what time of the month it is. She works hard and knows how to delegate for maximum productivity. (I would also guess that her children are not lazy.)

2. She is courageous.

She devotes herself wholeheartedly to her tasks. She may not feel qualified to do some of the things she does; she probably has to stretch outside of her comfort zone. Every task may not succeed, but she doesn't quit.

3. What she does is very important.

She has value. She does not wonder at night, as she lies in her bed, if anyone appreciates what she does. She has complete *job satisfaction*. She is fulfilled.

4. She promotes her husband in what she does.

She is a very valuable asset to him. He is thought of more highly because she is his wife. She does not compete with him or try to exceed him in his endeavors. She knows the power of their partnership.

5. She is selfless.

She does not *insist* on her personal "downtime". She does not *insist* on "doing things just for herself". There is no mention of her weekly "night out with the girls" or her day at the spa. She does not complain about her lot in life or her never ending responsibilities. We know this because she speaks with a kind spirit. She finds joy and refreshment in her role.

How do you measure up to our benchmark woman? I can tell you I have a long way to go! We can all learn a great deal from her. Commit yourself to the principles that govern her life. Look around you for other women that live out these principles in their lives. Surround yourself with them and glean what you can from them.

> *"As iron sharpens iron, so one man sharpens another" (Proverb 27:17).*

Be a "There YOU Are" Person

You are one of two types of people in this world: self-oriented or others-oriented. People will know when you walk into a room if you are a "Here I Am" person or a "There YOU Are" person. Which you are is made clear by your conversation, body language and actions. You are either drawing attention to yourself or giving your attention to others. It is obvious whether you are more concerned about yourself or other people.

> *"Be devoted to one another in brotherly love. Honor one another above yourselves" (Romans 12:10).*

It's often easy to love others, but honoring them above us requires effort and sometimes sacrifice. This doesn't mean you should belittle yourself and slink around like a lowly worm. Instead, it means you are so secure in yourself that you are free to appreciate others and build their esteem.

Treat others even better than you want to be treated. We do this not to manipulate others or to appear super-humble, but out of genuine love and concern. It's what being a Christian is all about!

"The greatest good we can do for others is not to share our riches but to reveal theirs."

-Author unknown

How do you build other people's self esteem? The answer is simple, not easy, but simple. *Talk about people's favorite subject: themselves.* People like to talk about themselves. Resist the urge to talk about yourself. Instead, talk about their interests and get them to share their stories. Be genuinely interested in them and what they say. Look them in the eye and show them you are listening. This shows that you care.

The art of conversation can be taught to any child or adult. It is best taught by example. Think of a person you know who makes you feel important when you talk with them. She has probably mastered the art of *You-oriented* conversation. *Self-oriented* conversation takes no effort or practice, since it is natural to talk about ourselves.

Gold Nugget:

Be a "There YOU Are" person. Focus on building others up instead of yourself.

The next time you are with *you-oriented* conversation-alists, observe how they listen and how they talk to you. How often do they sincerely compliment you and turn the conversation back to you?   Learn from their skills. You-oriented conversation puts people at ease and makes them feel important. Practice the fine art of good conversation.

Sincere Praise

Be stingy with your criticism and generous with your praise. When we criticize others, it makes people think less of us. They may wonder if we talk just as negatively about them behind their backs; and we probably do. If we are known for only saying positive things about others, people will begin to sincerely trust us. Give sincere praise as often as you can.

Gold Nugget:

People are starving for morsels of praise.

Sincere praise should not be confused with flattery used to manipulate people. It is simply showing sincere appreciation for the sake of encouraging another. We all receive too much criticism; it can weigh us down and crush our self-esteem. Isn't it amazing how one sincere compliment can counteract ten criticisms and brighten an otherwise gloomy day? People are starving for morsels of praise.

Take action. Say something positive, complimentary or encouraging to everyone you greet. It can be as simple as "I like your smile", "Your children are always so polite to me" or "You did a great job running the meeting today."

Walk away from gossip and criticism. Do you ever walk up on a conversation in which someone you know is being slandered? What do you do? The *easy* thing to do is to add your two-cents worth. The *hard* thing to do is to remain silent. The *noble* thing to do is to stop the conversation to protect that person's reputation and say only positive things about them in their absence. People will respect your integrity. Stand tall.

Personalities

Do you ever wonder, "Why do I act this way?" or "Why can't everyone be more like me?" Most of us don't understand why we act the way we do. We also have trouble understanding other people and getting along with them simply because we have different personalities. God chose to create each of us unique and special. It was no accident. Wouldn't it be boring if everyone thought and acted the same?

When I began to learn about the different personality types, I finally began to understand just *how* people differ in their basic make-up. We each typically fall into one of four basic personality styles based on whether we are more outgoing or reserved and more people-oriented or task-oriented. The four styles are typically designated as choleric (or D), sanguine (or I), phlegmatic (or S) and melancholy (or

C). These four types characterize how we are basically wired, but of course, we flex, change and grow.

Each of us has a set of strengths and weaknesses. You can use your weaknesses as excuses and think "well, that's just the way I am" or you can *change* for the better. The choice is *yours*.

When I took the time to learn about the different personality styles, I began to realize that I'm not really weird. The other people in my life aren't weird either; they are just different. As I learned a little more how to deal with each style, my people skills began to improve. I began to understand how my husband, children, parents and friends were all different. To be effective in my relationships, I must communicate differently with each person according to his personality style.

It is no surprise that most husbands and wives have opposite personality styles. Each one brings a unique set of strengths and weaknesses to the relationship that compliments and thus strengthens the partnership. Opposites often do attract!

For example, my husband's personality style likes clear, concise communication. The most effective method of communicating with him is the direct approach. Don't give him the fluffy details of what a big sale you found, whom you saw while shopping, what you had for lunch or how bad your feet hurt. Just tell him what he wants to know, the bottom line: "How much did you spend?"

Take the time to understand yourself, your family and your peers. Become an expert in personality styles. Desire to know how people work and how to more effectively communicate with them. When you adapt yourself to speak in a language they can understand, the static will fade from the transmission. It is a gift of love to take the time to understand people and communicate effectively with them. You can't change people, but you can change *you*.

Read a good book on personality styles and apply what you learn. (I recommend those by Florence Littauer, Dr. Robert Rohm, or Tim LaHaye.) You will be amazed at how your relationships with people will improve dramatically. You'll see they aren't really weird, just unique!

Gold Nugget:

It is a gift of love to take the time to understand people and communicate effectively with them. You can't change people, but you can change *you*.

Do What You Do Best

We were all created special by God. Each of us has her own unique personality, strengths, weaknesses, gifts and talents. We may not always like the package we have been given. But it was not our choice; it was a gift from our loving Creator. I hope your mother taught you to say "thank you" when you were given a gift. Stop right now and thank

God for the package He gave you.

We were not all given equal gifts. We may look at some people and think they have nothing special to offer, and yet look at others and wonder why they were blessed so much. It is obvious that we don't think like God thinks. In Isaiah 55:9, the Lord declares, *"As the heavens are higher than the earth, so are my ways higher than your ways and my thoughts higher than your thoughts."*

God must chuckle at our shortsighted judgement of His gift distribution. Remember God is perfect. God knows everything and made everything and everyone for a purpose. Who are we to question God, His gifts and those to whom He gave those gifts?

We all wish we could sing like so-and-so, were more outgoing like so-and-so or were more organized liked so-and-so. Realize that the package you were given to work with (your gifts and personality) was a gift from God to be used to serve Him.

What if you don't like the particular package you were given? Praise the Lord for it anyway, and then change what you can! God's relationship with us is all about molding us to be more like Christ. God can smooth off the roughest edges, tame the sharpest tongue, motivate the laziest soul and soften the hardest heart. He is an intimate God whose Holy Spirit works within us to accomplish His work through us. You don't doubt that God's work is important. Why would you doubt that your gifts and abilities to accomplish that work are important?

What did God give you? What do you do really well?

Are you really using it for Him? Or are you hiding it away for another time when you will feel more confident?

If you have the gift of hospitality, for example, do you have people into your home and meet the needs of others? If you are good at organizing and delegating, are you in a leadership position? If you have a servant's heart, are you helping behind the scenes?

A church Sunday School Class was searching for a secretary to handle attendance records and organize paperwork, etc. It was vital that this person be organized and dependable so those important things like visitors' names wouldn't fall through the cracks. The leadership struggled with whom to ask to do this job. The types of people who are good at this kind of job are typically not going to jump up and down asking where they can serve. The young lady that was asked to do the job was perfectly gifted to do it. In fact, she had been praying about a place to serve. She knew she had something to give, but she just didn't know where she could be useful. She got to do what *she did best*. If she had been asked to stand up in front of a class and take prayer requests, she would have passed out!

Let people do what they do best. If your husband is the detail-oriented organizer and you are the "I can't find my keys or my purse, but I like to talk" type, let him balance the checkbook and you make the phone calls for the upcoming party. Most likely you and your husband are opposite or at least very different in personality and gifts. It's almost as if God planned for couples to compliment and complete each other; it's not to drive us crazy. A marriage or any relationship will be stronger when each person is allowed to use his own gifts.

Gold Nugget:

A gift kept in the top of a closet might as well not have been given. Use the gifts God gave you.

You are excellent at doing something. Don't try to be like someone else. Don't compare yourself with others. Do what you are equipped to do.

Your Words

Control your conversation. Guard it. You alone are responsible for the words you say.

> *"With the tongue we praise our Lord and Father, and with it we curse men, who have been made in God's likeness. Out of the same mouth come praise and cursing. My brothers, this should not be" (James 3:9-10).*

Use your mouth for good wholesome talk and not for idle conversation. Let it be your greatest tool for building others up, not for tearing them down. If we truly are followers of Christ, our words as well as our actions should give us away. The world is watching and listening to you.

Good Manners

> *"Manners are like zero in arithmetic. They*
> *may not be much in themselves, but they are*
> *capable of adding a great deal of value to*
> *everything else."*
>
> *-Freya Stark*

Can you believe I am writing about manners in this book? I think they are so important. It is a way of showing *respect* to others. Using good manners and teaching them to our children is an excellent way of showing God's love to the world.

> *"Show respect for everyone. Love Christians*
> *everywhere. Fear God and honor the govern-*
> *ment" (I Peter 2:17 (TLB)).*

It is a good idea to read through an established book on etiquette. Yes, it is still applicable to our society today. You may find a dusty copy at the library or on a relative's bookshelf. First scan through it; you will find answers to many questions you had about dealing politely with people. Use it as a reference in the future. Don't think that etiquette is a list of stuffy, stifling rules for the rich and famous. We can all improve in our skills with people.

> *"A beautiful woman lacking discretion and*
> *modesty is like a fine gold ring in a pig's*
> *snout" (Proverbs 11:22(TLB)).*

Christians should be orderly and polite to demonstrate respect and love to others. Have you ever thought less of someone because they had good manners? Actually, people with good manners are usually more respected and trusted. They show a person has both humility and confidence.

Good manners are also a way to express your femininity. Men don't often take the initiative in this area. It is our job as women to exercise good manners and to teach them to our children. I admit that I am from the South, but good manners are universal and always enhance your femininity.

We can all improve on our skills with people and our manners. Here are a few basics:

1. Thank-you notes

Simply *write them*! Thank-you notes are appropriate for gifts or gestures that required someone's time, such as inviting you to dinner. They should be written within a few days. Notes need not be pretentious, stuffy or formal. They should be brief, sincere and written in your own simple words. If you have never been a thank-you note writer, start now. Also get your children in the habit of writing thank-you notes while they are young in hopes that it will be a life-long habit. (Thanks, Mom, for making me do this.)

2. Introductions

When you want to introduce two people, announce the name of the younger to the elder (or more respected person). Then introduce the elder to the younger. In this way, you show respect for age.

3. Table manners

Listed below are a few basic table manners. They are

not difficult to learn, but they make a big difference at the table. We must teach our children these simple courtesies; someday they will be grateful.

- Help pass dishes until everyone is served before you begin to eat.

- Don't talk while your mouth is full or take a bite when food is still in your mouth.

- Don't meet your food halfway with a rhythmic "ducking" motion. Bring your food to your mouth.

- Don't fuss with your appearance, i.e. comb hair or use makeup, at the table.

- Wait for everyone to finish before leaving the table. Sit and make pleasant conversation.

- Compliment the hostess and ask to be excused before leaving the table.

Critique yourself. How are your manners? If you want a really honest opinion, ask a trusted friend or your spouse. We all have room for improvement. Train your children in this area as a means of showing respect and serving others.

Be a Woman

Many women are afraid to be the very people they are created to be ... women. I am saddened that the feminist movement has duped women into thinking that being a woman is far inferior to *being* a man or being *like* a man. Did God in all His wisdom and grace create you to be a woman? Then *be* a woman.

I am not suggesting we should all dress in lacy skirts, wear pink bows in our hair and lilt about humming *"some day my prince will come."* But we should be **feminine**, which is simply defined as *having the qualities of a woman.* Being feminine is the *opposite* of being masculine, or like a man. This sounds elementary, but there is a vast difference between the two. Wasn't God clever in designing us different yet complementary?

Men are manly. It is man's nature to protect; a woman likes to be protected. How often throughout history have women banded together, leaving their husbands and children behind, grabbed weapons and defended their nation from injustice? Not too often. We have different qualities. A man likes the feminine qualities of a woman. Her tender heart, frailer body, softer voice, nurturing spirit and gentler ways are all very attractive to him.

1. Act like a woman.

A woman should not go around slapping people on the back, laughing from the gut, sitting unladylike, burping out loud or walking with a man's gait. These are not very becoming or feminine. Act like a lady, and you will command the respect of one.

2. Talk like a woman.

Do not try to lower your voice and talk like a man. Avoid coarse talk or jokes. These are very unbecoming and particularly inappropriate for women. Do not go out of your way to be the loudest or funniest person in a group. Edify others with your conversation and practice listening more than you talk.

3. Look like a woman.

Avoid wearing men's clothes, styles or fabrics. If you prefer masculine styles, make sure the details or fabrics are feminine. You can look feminine even in your most rugged hiking gear.

Avoid revealing, too-tight or too-short clothes; they are distasteful and not feminine. Your wardrobe, hair, jewelry and make-up should enhance your inner beauty, not detract from your feminine character.

Looking, talking, and acting feminine is timelessly beautiful, fashionable and always appropriate for a woman.

Chapter 7
Dare to Love Your Man

Godly Marriages

Are you discouraged about the negative aura surrounding the concept of marriage today? We see people enter this sacred partnership without the commitment God intended. Infidelity and "I've lost that loving feeling" seem to melt marriages quicker than butter on a baked potato. Yet I am amazed that so many young people still genuinely want a lasting marriage. They just need to know "how" to have one. In the nightstand of every honeymoon suite lies the instruction book for a godly marriage: *The Bible*.

Do not be fooled into thinking that marriage as God intended it to be is a thing of the past, or that marriage today is different than it was for my grandmother's generation. Nonsense! Every month godly marriages are springing up as a result of young people who are seizing the marriage commitment for life. Many of them grew up in families where they knew that, for mom and dad, divorce was not an option. Others did not have this example in their home, but learned the picture of biblical marriage later in life.

Gold Nugget:

In the nightstand of every honeymoon suite lies the instruction book for a godly marriage: *The Bible*.

The marriage of friends Joe and Angi greatly influenced me. There's no doubt that this young couple love the Lord as they openly proclaimed their faith in God and acceptance of His design for marriage. The wedding ceremony included the story of their relationship. Their intimate thoughts and feelings were revealed from their first meeting through the proposal and wedding. As the history of their relationship was read aloud during the ceremony, we learned what attracted them to each other, what they admired about each other and how they knew that this relationship was God's will. What a precious thing to have on the wedding video - *a proclamation of their devotion and intent for marriage.* I had never seen such a touching ceremony.

Let's all try to remember... What were those things that attracted you to your husband? What were the things about him you could not live without? Why did you choose your spouse above all others? *Focus* on those things. *Tell* him those things (again and again).

Will Joe and Angi have struggles? Sure they will; we all do. If any of you don't, please write to me. The trials of marriage can burn away the junk in our lives and leave a purer relationship, or they can leave us bitter and bruised. I pray that Joe and Angi will watch their wedding video often and be reminded of their commitment. I believe their marriage will touch thousands of others.

Thank you, Lord, for this young generation that is unashamedly committed to you and your plan for marriage. Protect them. Nurture them. Guide them. Help us to set a shining example for them.

Gold Nugget:

**Why did you choose your
spouse above all others?
Focus on those things.
Tell him those things
(again and again).**

The Pizza Man

Has a pizza deliveryman ever inspired you? In the midst of writing this book, I ordered a pizza for dinner. The deliveryman, a 60-year-old gentleman, greeted me at the door with a sweet smile and kind words. He said, "Your name reminds me of my wife." I looked puzzled. He continued, "*LaFlam* means '*the flame*', and I have a flame burning bright for my wife. You see, we've only been married for thirty-four years." He was so sincere and excited about his wife. I felt like giving him a hug. I also wanted to meet his *incredible* wife.

Three months later, I *did* meet the pizza man's wife. This time I was picking up my pizza from the same shop. There at the counter stood a cute, joyful, silver-haired lady *flirting* with "the pizza man" like they were sixteen-year-olds! (I knew immediately who she was.) How romantic! It was obvious that she still had a flame burning brightly for her husband of thirty-four years. Her love was evident in the special way she looked at him.

Wouldn't we all like our husbands to say they had *flames burning brightly* for us? What an unexpected blessing from a pizza delivery. May we all say after thirty-four years of marriage that we still have flames burning brightly for each other.

You Married a Man

Of course he is a man; that's why you married him. You were attracted to his manliness: his masculine voice, body, mannerisms and character. But when you married him, you may not have realized all the other things that go along with being a man. He is different from you in many more areas than the obvious physical differences.

Let's face it, he eats more. A trendy green salad just won't fill him up at dinner. *But don't you love feeding him a dinner that satisfies his "Hungry Jack" appetite?*

He sweats more and probably uses more clothes than you each day. Since his clothes are bigger, this results in more loads of laundry. *But don't you love cuddling up in his big shirt or, better yet, his big strong arms?*

He takes up more space in the bed and often makes strange sleeping noises. You sleep quietly, always on your side of the bed. *But aren't you glad he's there to hold and protect you?*

He speaks louder (and needs the television louder). You speak softly and can hear the television on mute. *But don't you love how he speaks with authority?*

He would rather have his chest hairs plucked than go shopping. *But aren't you glad he doesn't follow you around all day shopping and brag about how much money he saved at the big sales?*

He likes (*or maybe adores*) sports (*of any kind*). He likes action (*and hates romance*) movies. He enjoys camping without a shower or shave for three days. He likes looking at cars and driving fast. You may not enjoy any of these things. *But wouldn't it be weird if your husband liked to talk all day about recipes, hairstyles and which pants make his hips look slimmer?*

Gold Nugget:

You married a man. He is different than you. Accept it and enjoy it.

You Can't Change Him

A woman often enters marriage thinking her Prince Charming is perfect. After a few weeks or months she realizes that he is <u>not</u>. In fact she may create a prioritized list entitled "Things I Want to Change about My Husband" and then develop a strategic action plan to accomplish these changes. Not willing to accept the fact that she can't change her husband, she becomes frustrated. This leads to anger, bitterness and strife. This does not make a peaceful home.

> *"Keep thy eyes wide open before marriage,*
> *and half-shut afterwards."*
>
> *-Benjamin Franklin*

Do you truly want peace and freedom in your home? Write these simple words on your heart until they sink in: **YOU CAN'T CHANGE HIM, SO DON'T EVEN TRY**. You may be saying, "But you don't know my husband!" No I don't, but you picked him.

We rationalize, "I only want to *help* him" or "I only point out his faults because I really *love* him." We often justify our nagging by claiming to only give him *constructive* criticism.

Focus on his *strengths*. What do you admire and love about him? Begin praising him (*yes, out loud*) for those things. Tell him how proud you are of his accomplishments, or how you feel so safe being with him, or how his smile makes you melt or whatever you truly adore about him. If you speak these things to him, you will start to believe in your heart what you are speaking. You will say, "Wow, what a great man I have!" I dare you to try this. You'll see for yourself how your relationship improves.

> *"Most of us would rather be ruined by praise
> than saved by criticism."*

> *-Norman Vincent Peale*

Concerning criticism - there is no *constructive* criticism, only *destructive*. Nagging will wear even the most confident man down and build a wall between you. Men face a lot of criticism in the workplace and among their peers. Sometimes the toughest guys have the most fragile egos. Nothing can build up or tear down a man's self-image like a woman's words. Choose your words wisely. Build him up. Don't ever worry that he might get an ego. He needs to have your confidence, respect and encouragement. It's for your own good.

The secret to peace in your marriage relationship is to accept your husband 100% just as he is. Yes, with all his faults and bad habits. Remember that he could make an equally long list of your shortcoming. Ask God to help you overlook his faults. You may not accept or approve of everything he does, but you can accept *him*.

> *"...Love does not demand its own way. It is
> not irritably or touchy. It does not hold
> grudges and will hardly even notice when
> others do it wrong"* (I Corinthians 13:5
> (TLB)).

At your wedding you proclaimed some very powerful words of commitment before God, your spouse, your family and friends. Did you really mean them? I hope so. Do you act like it?

True love is not conditional nor is it always emotionally pleasing. The kind of love you spoke in your vows is a "committed-no-matter-what" kind of love, like Christ's love for the church. Accepting your husband will *free* you to really love him. He needs the security of your unconditional love. Aren't you glad God's love for us is unconditional? Imagine what your display of unconditional love could mean in your family.

Gold Nugget:

Accepting your husband as he is will bring unexplainable freedom into your life.

Oneness

> *"For this reason a man will leave his father and mother and be united to his wife, and they will become one flesh"* (Genesis 2:24).

Great marriages have a spirit of oneness about them. Not just unity and harmony, not just getting along, but a true adventurous spirit of "it's just us against the world". After all, you liked him so much that you said "no" to all others to begin this lifelong quest called marriage. Within this spirit of oneness lies all the freedom and joys of marriage.

When I started dating my husband-to-be, one of the things

that attracted me (understatement) was his incredible *vision*. I said immediately, "I like this man's vision and I want to be a part of his life". I found the person with whom I wanted to be *one*. Thankfully, he invited me to be his life partner. We share this spirit of oneness; it's indescribable.

A Family Purpose

A spirit of oneness is worthless unless you are going somewhere and doing something. Each family, that is each husband and wife, must have a purpose. Have a vision of what you want to become and where you want to go.

If you could visualize your family in five years, ten years or twenty years, what would it be like? What would you be doing? What would you have accomplished? What would your relationships be like? What impact would you have had on the world? What dreams would you have fulfilled?

It's often hard to get a man to talk about his vision for the future. He may not verbalize his plans so as not to risk failure. Or, even worse, he may fear someone laughing at his dreams. It is one thing for his buddies at work to criticize him, but when his wife does, it cuts to the core of his heart. He may resist ever sharing such personal thoughts again. He may even resist any communication with his wife.

Determine your family's purpose. Develop a vision for your family. Let him know of your undying commitment to him and the vision God has given him. Let your spirit of oneness hold you close as you pursue your life dreams together.

Gold Nugget:

Have a vision of what you want to become and where you want to go as a family.

You + Me = a Team

Have you ever seen a member of the Dallas Cowboys intentionally tackling another player on his own team? Of course not. They are on the same team with the same goal - to win every game they play. Why then do we intentionally try to hurt, destroy or compete with members of our team - our own family? It makes no sense.

Do you believe that your family is stronger than the individual members are? Consider a three-ply cord versus three individual strands. The three-ply cord is many times stronger than the sum of the individual cords. It's no mistake that each ply of the cord is positioned in the same direction as the other cords and then wrapped tightly together. There is no strength (or usefulness) when each ply is crossing the others.

We are as foolish as criss-crossed strands of a cord when we are petty about getting our own way, avenging wrongs and always having to have the last word. We must grow up. We must function as a team.

We all know that members of a team have to give and take and accept the weaknesses of each team member. Team players don't hurt or destroy each other. They build each other up and encourage one another to be their best.

> *"Bear with each other and forgive whatever grievances you may have against one another. Forgive as the Lord forgave you. And over all these virtues put on love, which binds them all together in perfect unity"* (Colossians 3:13-14).

The next time you are having an argument with your husband, stop and think, "We are on the same team." Hmmm. Is the argument still worth having? Probably not. Bear with him. Forgive him. Support him. Encourage him. Try to understand him. Be his best friend. You are probably the best friend he will ever have; and he can be yours.

Gooooooo Team!!!!

Cheer for Him

> *"If you love someone you will be loyal to him no matter what the cost. You will always believe in him, always expect the best of him, and always stand your ground in defending him"* (I Corinthians 13:7 (TLB)).

Be enthusiastic about your husband's interests. He will be delighted that you care about what he is interested in. Maybe you detest golf, fishing, cars, computers or whatever he is interested in, but at least respect his love for them. Often, men do not want their wives' participation, but they do want their respect and approval. Golf and fishing are probably more fun with his buddies, but he wants his wife to appreciate his affection for these things. They are part of *who* he is.

Share his dreams. Has your husband ever shared with you any dream he wants to accomplish in life that he couldn't tell anyone else because it sounds too crazy? If so, be thankful, you have a healthy relationship. He trusts you with his most intimate thoughts.

How did you respond when he shared his dream? Did you laugh, scoff, criticize and tell him why he could never do it? Or did you encourage, support and offer to help? If you don't believe in him, support him or cheer for him, who else will? He yearns to hear you say, "You can do it! I believe in you."

My husband shared with me his dream of running the New York City Marathon (*26 miles of fun*) before he reached age thirty. I was not convinced he could do it, since he had never run more than six miles at one time. I tried to be supportive throughout training by filling his water bottles, washing his sweaty clothes and not complaining (too often) about the long Saturday morning training runs. Surprisingly, I was one of his few supporters. Most people were negative and critical about his pursuit of one of his lifelong dreams. (It's funny how critical people can be when someone pursues something great.)

Twenty-nine days before his thirtieth birthday, with much persistence and courage, HE DID IT! He dared to dream and then valiantly pursued his dream. I was so proud of him all along the way. I feel like I contributed in a small way to his achievement. The whole experience brought us closer; it's hard to explain.

Gold Nugget:

A man just needs to know that his wife is on his team cheering for him even if the game hasn't started yet.

A man is so sensitive to his wife's opinion. He is stifled if she has a critical spirit. Tiny criticisms may crush his ego so that he refuses to share any more intimate dreams. A wise woman supports her husband's dreams because she supports him. Share his dreams. Be his best cheerleader. Rah! Rah! Rah!

Please Your Man

Do you remember how hard you tried to please your husband-to-be when you were dating? You remembered which outfits he commented on, which hairstyle he liked and which perfume he noticed. You spent so much thought and effort trying to please your man. You focused on what he liked. This effort was an expression of your love and devotion to him.

Shortly after I got married, I forgot to maintain the effort of pleasing him. I reverted back to what I wanted and what made me happy, totally disregarding what my husband really liked. I guess I claimed to be trying to please him, but I really was not.

I began to dress to please myself instead of him. I wore

clothes that were more comfortable rather than the fitted, more tailored style that he preferred. Oh yes, he noticed.

And why did I continue to cook rice for dinner after he told me he didn't like it? My disregard for his desires must have been a slap in the face, although he rarely spoke out about it.

My greatest lack of consideration was my hairstyle. I like to change hairstyles with the seasons. No two pictures of me have the same hairstyle. He liked my hair long, like it was when we met. I kept it this way for a couple of years, but then was seduced by those cute, shorter styles. I felt it was flattering to my thin face and much more stylish.

Then after having children... need I say more... a girl has to have that "I-don't-have-time-to-do-hair" hairstyle. Aren't those styles flattering with those part-partum pounds, "I-can't-get-back-into-my-real-clothes" wardrobe, and that "I-was-up-all-night-and-didn't-feel-like-wearing-make-up" face? After one look at me, I doubt my husband was thinking, "Wow, what a beautiful bride I married". It was more like, "What happened to that girl I married?" Don't get me wrong, my husband is not concerned about my looking perfectly made-up all the time. In fact he says his favorite "look" is when I have taken my make-up off at night and changed into my cozy pajamas.

My husband would never get angry about my visits to the salon, but always mentioned that he liked my hair longer. After nine years of marriage, I finally realized, "Duh, I guess I should wear my hair the way he likes it." *Whom do I want to please*: my friends, other men or my husband? The answer is obvious. Marriage was so much sweeter after I submitted in this minor area. I may not look so chic, but I do love those compliments from my man.

I began to realize that if I really want to be an excellent wife I should try to please my man. I want him to be proud of who I am. I want to do things for him each day to let him know he's still my #1 choice. Let's flip the coin. Don't we love it when our husbands make a special effort to please us?

Gold Nugget:

**Do things for him each day
to let him know he's still
your #1 choice.**

When He Comes Home From Work

When your husband comes home from work, he needs to be welcomed into his peaceful, loving home. He needs to know that no matter how bad things are at work, his home is a haven where he is always welcome. Even if people don't treat him with the respect he deserves in his profession, he will be treated with respect in his own home.

Many women demand that their husbands come home from work and immediately start doing chores to help them out around the house. Particularly, stay-at-home moms may think their husbands come home to relieve them of all their duties. When he walks through the door, he may find the kids are screaming, the house is a wreck, dinner hasn't been given a thought and his bride unloads what a terrible day she has experienced. She hits him immediately with the gripes of the day and then spouts off a list of things he can do to help her. If I were this husband, I would get in the car and go back to work.

If you are home before your husband arrives, do your best to have your home in order. This may sound old-fashioned or even impossible. I remember my mom making a special effort to do this. Try to have the house quiet, the toys picked up, the kids calm, yourself presentable and dinner at least planned. A man needs to walk into his home and feel like it is his *paradise,* not his nightmare. He needs to know that at least this area of his life is really great. You would be surprised how important this is to a man.

A little effort before he arrives may work wonders for his ego. I'm not suggesting you to fetch his slippers and feed him grapes, but he needs to know you are happy caring for him. He is not coming home to serve you. You are there to serve him. The wife is the helpmate. The husband is the head of the home.

Gold Nugget:

Treat him like he is the head of the home, and he will act like it.

Listen up, ladies. Here comes an important one!

Quiet, Please!

It is our nature as women to unload the 10,000 words we have been saving up all day in the first thirty minutes our husband is home. *Save your words.* Exercise some self-control with your conversation. He probably prefers a little quiet after his busy day. Put yourself in his shoes. Think how you can serve him, not how he can serve you. If you don't immediately bombard him with your words, he may actually want to use a few of his own words and tell you what is on his mind.

Gold Nugget:

If we want our husbands to talk with us more, we must first *be quiet* and *listen*.

The "S" Word

No, this section is not about sex. Sorry to disappoint you. It's about ... **submission**. "Oh, no!" you say, "Not another woman beating me over the head to submit to my big lug of a husband!"

> *"You wives, submit yourselves to your husbands, for that is what the Lord has planned for you" (Colossians 3:18 (TLB)).*

We hate to hear it, but we know it's right, because the Bible commands us to submit to our husbands. Our sinful nature causes us to reject authority of any kind. We resist submitting to God or any person. Need I say more? Submission is a Christ-honoring quality. It requires humility and self-control.

> *"Honor Christ by submitting to each other"*
> *(Ephesians 5:21 (TLB)).*

A woman may get chills up her spine when she hears instruction about submission for a number of reasons:

1. She thinks this command is to make her feel inferior to or less valuable than her husband.

Not true. There has to be one leader; I don't know of a corporation that has two CEO's or an Indian tribe that has two chiefs. She feels if she truly submitted to him, he would take advantage of her and develop an ego that would be impossible to bear.

2. She does not respect his leadership.

I have heard so many women say, "If only my husband would be a man and *lead* me, then I would follow him." Many of these ladies are not allowing their husbands to lead them. Instead, they are *"wearing all the pants"* in the household so there are none left for him to put on. Ladies, it actually works the other way. If we politely hang those figurative "pants" in the closet and put on a figurative "skirt", he will (and he really wants to) wear the pants.

3. She is not submitting to God.

> *"You wives must submit to your husbands'*
> *leadership in the same way you submit to the*

Lord" (Ephesians 5:22 (TLB)).

When we are not submitting to God, we have a difficult time obeying a command like this one requiring us to submit to another person. When we truly love God and accept that His plan for us is best, we will desire to obey this command. Why would God require this of us and not equip us to carry it out? It is possible with the Holy Spirit's help. You can do it!

What Is Submission?

Many women were not raised by mothers who exemplified godly submission. Thankfully, I was. I can speak from my upbringing that biblical submission is a beautiful thing. Let's first look at what submission is not.

Submission is not:

- Inferiority, or being second-rate
- Refraining from family discussions
- Total absence from the decision-making process (But the final decision does belong to him.)
- Openness to abuse

Submission is:

- Respecting physical differences between man and woman

- Serving him out of your love and commitment

- Acknowledging that his authority over you comes from God

- Yielding to his authority (without whining and complaining)

- Respecting him as the head visionary, planner and provider

- Upholding and enforcing his authority over the children

- Supporting his decisions concerning jobs, homes, spiritual life, budget, children, family, social activities, etc.

- Setting an example for children to respect and obey authority

Many disagree that this is how marriages should operate these days. The "50/50 philosophy" is so popular in our culture. Remember that the Designer of marriage wrote the guidelines for us, and He truly wants us to succeed.

Chapter 8
Dare to Excel in Your Work

"She watches over the affairs of her house-hold and does not eat the bread of idleness"
(Proverbs 31:27).

What Do You Do?

After introducing yourself to a new person, the next question typically asked is "what do you *do*?" When we ask this question, we mean, "what is your profession or job?" "*What*" a person does is a big part of who they are.

What do *you* do? Do you have a job outside your home? Do you work inside your home? Everyone *does* something. Are you a professional homemaker or stay-at-home mom? Are you a student or a professional grandmother? Whatever it is that you do, the same work principles apply to you.

Your occupation tells a great deal about how you spend

your time and with whom you associate. But people are so much more than what they do for a living. Each person is an *individual* with a multitude of abilities and a variety of opportunities. Jesus was the master at seeing the person inside above his occupation, outer appearance or status in life.

It is hard for us to see the dreams and potential inside a person. I know of an elementary school dropout who swept floors as a janitor before he realized his potential and became the CEO of his own successful company that helped change people's lives. He had the courage and diligence to pursue his dream despite his circumstances.

Work Hard - Lose the Laziness

> *"Lazy hands make a man poor, but diligent hands bring wealth" (Proverbs 10:4).*

> *"This should be your ambition: to live a quiet life, minding your own business and doing your own work, just as we told you before. As a result, people who are not Christians will trust and respect you, and you will not need to depend on others for enough money to pay your bills" (1 Thessalonians 4:11-12 (TLB)).*

God did not create man to be lazy, but to work and rule over the earth. In 1 Thessalonians, Paul made it clear that Christians should not be loafers. He set the example by working hard to earn his own living, not depending on others.

If you are lazy or associate with lazy people, watch out!

Idleness can only lead to trouble, discouragement and even poverty. Work hard at what you do. Strive for continuous improvement.

Gold Nugget:

**Don't ever think you are
the best that you can be.**

If you are a homemaker or a stay-at-home mom, you too must keep busy doing your job. You may not drive to work everyday or receive a paycheck, but your work is vital to your family and to the Lord. Excel at what you do, find better ways to do your job and make sure your time is spent doing the truly important things. See how much you can encourage and bless those around you.

Your Best

Do you really do your *best* at your job? Do you do *more than is expected*? If you were your boss, would you be pleased with your performance? Whether you are waiting tables or performing brain surgery, your work should be pleasing to the Lord. Imagine that Jesus is literally your boss (because He really is your ultimate authority). After all, He created you, gave you the ability to work, gave you the opportunity and gives you the monetary rewards.

> *"Whatever you do, work at it with all your
> heart, as working for the Lord, not for men,*

since you know that you will receive an inheritance from the Lord as a reward. It is the Lord Christ you are serving" (Colossians 3:23-24).

A job or profession is more than just a means of earning money. Certainly it is a practical means by which our physical needs are met. It is also a living testimony back to the Lord. Yes, God is very interested in what we do from "9 to 5". We represent Him wherever we go.

God expects us to act like Christians even in our work. That means honoring and esteeming others, submitting to authority, serving others and exercising the character of Christer.   Christ's character includes love, forgiveness, kindness, compassion, gentleness, integrity, peace and wisdom. These same characteristics should exude from our lives via the power of the Holy Spirit within us.

Using Your Time

I had the privilege of having one job where my employer billed my time to individual clients. Most consultants, accountants and attorneys also bill clients for the hours spent working for them. I was responsible for keeping track of each quarter of an hour that I worked for each client.

Billing my time was a great exercise in using every minute at work wisely. For every hour I billed a client, I wanted to make sure that I had done a fair job that was worth the rate he would be charged. Wasting a half-hour here and there was either wasting my client's or my employer's money. At the end of every day, I wanted to make sure I had given a good effort and earned my billable rate.

When you are at work, try to think about work (not home) so that when you are at home, you can think about home (not work). Maintain a high level of productivity, even when the boss isn't watching.

> *"Slaves, obey your earthly masters in everything; and do it, not only when their eye is on you and to win their favor, but with sincerity of heart and reverence for the Lord" (Colossians 3:22).*

I have had people working for me who only did the minimum, or what was expected. These people worked hard while I was around, but I knew their behavior changed when I wasn't.

I have also had employees who did above and beyond what I expected, because they had something courageous inside of them that commanded them to always do their best. They weren't so concerned if I was watching them, because they were not just working to please me. They had a higher authority and noble character.

Integrity

It is no secret that dealing honestly and fairly with people is pleasing to the Lord. He expects us to display utmost integrity in our work. Most of us would never consider stealing from our employer. But what about taking home office supplies, loafing on the job or taking long lunches without making up the time? These are more subtle ways we can steal.

Think about how you would feel if you were the company owner and every employee worked like you. Would the company be more successful or less?

Gold Nugget:

Would your workplace be better if everyone worked like you?

Work hard to protect your good name. Be known as a person of integrity, an example for others to follow even when it is not convenient. Doing the right things may be difficult at times, but we serve the Lord, not our flesh.

> *"A good name is more desirable than great riches; to be esteemed is better than silver or gold" (Proverbs 22:1).*

Responsibility

I have often heard that people get paid for the *responsibility* they assume. The more a person is responsible for, the more he will get paid. For example, a restaurant manager is ultimately responsible for the food, service, maintenance, customer satisfaction and every other aspect of his business. He must be willing to serve in any capacity needed; this may even mean sweeping the floor or washing dishes. He's probably the first person to arrive and the last person to leave every night. It makes sense that he makes more money than the waitress and the dishwasher who have much less responsibility.

If you want to make more money, whining about it or wishing for it won't get it. You must first assume more *responsibility*. If you are incapable of assuming more responsibility, you must grow, change and train yourself until you are capable.

If you own your own business, you understand that you are ultimately responsible for everything (good or bad). No one has to tell the business owner to get to work on time. He does so because he is responsible for the outcome of his business.

I started working in a retail shop when I was fourteen. It was a great experience working with several entrepreneurial owners. I watched the owners make the difficult daily decisions, deal with angry customers and manage the employees. I learned that assuming responsibility takes a great deal of *courage*. A couple years later, the owner left me solely in charge of the store for a week when she went on vacation. I saw that responsibility wasn't very glamorous, but hard work. I loved the challenge; this opened the door for future opportunities to assume more responsibility.

Your Attitude at Work

Do you know people where you work who are always

griping that they are underpaid and overworked? They have no respect for their superiors; they don't trust anyone and constantly criticize people and decisions made. I hope you are not one of these people. How would you like to run a business with employees like these?

These people with chronic bad attitudes have a "victim mentality". They think everyone is against them, have no control over their lives and whine that life is unfair. These people have a poor self-image and a sad outlook on life; they are unwilling to accept responsibility for their lives. Since this attitude is contagious, my advice is to minimize association with them. If your company is full of them, you may want to consider moving on ... to a more positive environment.

> *"I've never seen a monument erected to a pessimist."*
>
> *- Paul Harvey*

If you are a Christian, your attitude at work should give you away and shine out from among the sea of poor attitudes. It should be radically different than those around you. Here's how:

- Be respectful and compliant with those in authority over you.

- Be kind and considerate to those subject to you.

- Be a solution-seeker, not a faultfinder or a finger-pointer.

- Do more than is expected of you.
  Don't think the company owes you
  more.

- Expect to prosper if you work and plan
  for it.

- Be thankful for your job, your income
  and your employer.

It's All About People

Relationships are *everything* in the workplace. It is to your advantage as well as the success of your company to build good work relationships. Take the time to understand your co-workers, employees and customers. Develop good listening skills. Think in terms of helping *them* succeed in their job; this will most likely help you succeed in yours.

Gold Nugget:

Maintain a win-win
attitude.

---

*"Motivate them, train them, care about them
and make winners out of them..."*

- J.W. Marriot, Jr.

Avoid gossip and criticism. Nothing undermines and weakens the workplace like negative talk. It wastes time, money and energy that could otherwise be spent productively.

Gold Nugget:

Use every opportunity you can to give a person a "pat on the back".

Build others up. The best kinds of "pats on the back" are verbal. Give verbal praise when people do a great job. Don't just tell the person one-on-one. It's great to praise people in front of others, especially their superiors.

You may even want to write a letter to the person's boss expressing your appreciation of their extra effort. People need to know when they excel. Morale can soar. Wouldn't you love to own a company where employees encouraged each other instead of "stabbing each other in the back"?

Zig Ziglar says, *"You can have everything you want in life if you just help enough other people get what they want."* Zig is right. When you give and bless others, you will be blessed. The workplace is full of people who are just looking out for themselves with no concern for others. People want to work with coworkers who help them, encourage them and genuinely care about their success. If our efforts to support others are genuine, without expecting anything in return, our co-workers will trust us.   As Christians, we should be a light among the world in which we live and work. It should be evident that we are full of Christ's love.

Working with Men

Ladies, this is a very important topic for the workplace. As Christian women we must commit to purity in our relationships with co-workers. In a society where adulterous relationships are common and often accepted, we must stand firm to live holy lives as God commands.

When I was working in the engineering field, I worked almost entirely with men. As a single and later married woman, I understand the challenges associated with working with men.

Here are some practical guidelines to keep pure relationships with men in the workplace:

- Avoid dining/traveling alone with another male co-worker.

- Dress conservatively. Avoid tight, revealing or suggestive clothing.

- Walk away from crude or improper conversation.

- Don't flirt. Even the slightest remarks can encourage men.

- Only discuss work-related issues with men. There is little place for outside conversation. This can help avoid becoming "good friends" with other men at work.

- If you are getting too close to another man, stop it immediately and maintain strictly business contact with him.

Gold Nugget:

As Christian women we must commit to purity in our relationships with men in the workplace.

Above all guard yourself against immorality. Do not be so foolish to think that you are immune from temptation. You will experience it, and you must be prepared to run from it. Be assured that God is on your side helping you.

> *"...And God is faithful; he will not let you be tempted beyond what you can bear. But when you are tempted, he will also provide a way out so that you can stand up under it" (1 Corinthians 10:13).*

Performance Evaluation

It's time to evaluate your *work performance*. You may do this periodically with your employer as well as with your employees. Take a minute to honestly answer the following questions. Let them prompt you to think about what work you do and how you do it.

- How do you feel about "what you do"? Are you proud of it? Are you embarrassed or insecure about it?

- Are you excited about doing your work? Is it what you planned to do?

- Are you consumed with your job? Do you find it difficult to separate yourself from your work?

- Are you good at your work? Did you train for a long time to do it? Do you have a great deal of experience? Are you continually improving?

- If you are not doing what you really want to do, why not? What holds you back?

- Does your work hinder your family? Does your work hinder your Christian witness?

Seek the Lord for guidance in these issues. God really does care about your work. It is important to Him. Many people think they can only approach God about what we perceive as "spiritual" things. God is concerned about every aspect of your life.

Gold Nugget:

God really does care about your work.

Stewardship

God has blessed each of us far more than we can imagine. We deserve nothing, and He gives us every spiritual blessing and material things as well. Take a moment to thank Him. Then ask Him to help you always be a faithful steward.

Gold Nugget:

God gives to givers so that they can give away and always acknowledge Him as the Giver.

Are you a good steward? Are you fully using all that you have been given the way the Lord wants you to use it?

Chapter 9

Dare to Have a Happy Home

Manage the Home

A woman is typically responsible for managing the affairs of her household. This can include most purchases, meal preparation, laundry and cleaning, social planning, care for children, etc. Whether she does it all herself or delegates it to family members or hired help, it is her responsibility to make sure that all of these things are done. Some of you may be saying, "This isn't fair; my husband's list of responsibilities is shorter than mine."

I know that many of you women are also providing financially for your families. Does this get you off the hook for managing the affairs of your home?   Not exactly. Remember the wise woman in Proverbs 31? She was skillful at delegation. She ran her business and her home well. Nothing was overlooked.

Managing the home is a privilege. It is an opportunity to

express yourself. Your home and family will reflect *YOU*, *your character* and *your personality*. This is a gift from God and a source of blessing to your family.

You can express your creativity even through the subtle details in your home. For example, what man would notice how nicely the striped pillows on the sofa compliment your floral window treatment, or how cleverly you sneaked in some vitamin C and fiber when you added broccoli to the casserole? It is the thoughtful little things you do everyday that often go unnoticed that bless your family.

God gave women the special ability to nurture and care for people. There is no one more comforting to a sick child than his mother. Nothing remedies homesickness like mother's home cooking. Generously use your gift of nurturing with your family.

Women were made to shop smart. I have never seen a man that could surpass a woman's ability to be creatively thrifty when meeting the needs of her family. Little things, like buying the children's clothes for next year during the end-of-the-season sales, can help any family stay within their budget. Finances can be prime material for arguments in the home. Your efforts to live within the budget are a tangible sign of your submission to your husband in this area. No matter what your income level or lifestyle, your thriftiness will please your husband.

Women also have an amazing ability to do a million things at once. Do you know a man who can feed a baby, talk on the phone, cook supper and call out spelling words at the same time? I don't think so. Men typically need to focus more on one task at a time.

My husband is still astonished at how I can think through all the possible needs of my family for a week of vacation. We rarely forget a thing, even the first aid kit - just in case. (However, there was that one trip when I packed only his French cuff shirts and *NO* cuff links. Oops!)

Ladies, your ability to manage the home is *so* important. There are so many things to take care of and you can lovingly oversee it all. You are amazing women!

Inside Your Home

Now let's talk about inside your home - your actual living space. Do you *generally* keep it neat and orderly? If you walked into my house unannounced, it would certainly not be magazine photo perfect, but I probably would not be embarrassed either.

I struggle with details and organization. (I would rather just "wing it".) I need lists to accomplish anything in life, or I just wander aimlessly never sure if I do anything important. One thing that changed my life was a simple tool: a household chore checklist. You organized-types are laughing at my simplicity now. This simple tool enables me to check off each chore as I do it weekly. Otherwise I wonder, "Did I wash the sheets this week?"

Is your home a place where your family loves to be and guests feel comfortable? Your home doesn't have to be professionally decorated to be beautiful and comfortable. Do the best you can with your budget and lifestyle.

You can become a self-educated decorator for free. Go to the public library or a bookstore and look at decorating magazines. No need to buy them, just write down or photocopy ideas you like. There are so many simple ways you can inexpensively improve your home. If you don't know where to start, ask a friend whose home you find appealing to give you some suggestions.

Gold Nugget:

Your home and family will reflect YOU, your character and your personality.

Homemaking Today

What comes to mind when you think of a *homemaker*? She is probably featured in a movie from the 1940's where a woman's goal in life was to marry, raise children and be a housewife. She sports a cotton house dress and apron while she glides around the kitchen preparing delicious homemade (there were no store-bought) meals, totally fulfilled in caring for her spotless home and unselfishly meeting the needs of her husband and children. She takes pride in her chosen profession and is totally fulfilled. She learned this trade from her mother and grandmother and, of course, made an A in Home Economics. Not only can she sew on a button, but she can hem pants and iron cotton shirts too. After a long day of household chores, she relaxes by reading the latest edition of

Better Homes and Gardens to get new ideas for improving her home life.

You may be saying, "Ha! This is not the 40's and I am not Martha Stewart!" You are right. Things have changed, and Martha has a huge staff of professionals working for her. Women have modified their role over the past decades. More women have pursued education, careers and personal interests often at a higher priority than their families. Can we say that our society has improved because of these changes? Have we raised better children? Have we equipped young women to live godly lives and raise godly families? I am not so sure that we have.

If you ask young women today what they want to be when they grow up, few would say they want to be *homemakers*. Young ladies are receiving a message loud and clear that being "just a homemaker" is not a worthy ambition and pales in comparison to other careers. This is a tragedy.

What can we do? Plenty. Whether or not you work outside your home, do your job (of homemaking) well. Your excellent work in your home will be a testimony to your family and the world that you are God's woman fulfilling your God-given role. Spread the message that the career of homemaking is fulfilling and important. Train your daughters in the arts and sciences of homemaking, so that they will be equipped if they choose this noble profession. Whether or not you are a homemaker, encourage the homemakers that you know; they rarely receive any recognition or praise. They need to know that what they do is an important profession.

Homemaking as a Profession

> *"These older women must train the younger women to live quietly, to love their husbands and their children, and to be sensible and clean minded, spending their time in their own homes, being kind and obedient to their husbands, so that the Christian faith can't be spoken against by those who know them"* *(Titus 2:4-5 (TLB).*

Homemaking is still indeed a noble profession. It is full of challenges and opportunities for achievement. It requires ambition and cross-functional skills. It is for the self-motivated and the determined. The rewards are sometimes unseen, but they are substantial and often eternal.

When I graduated from college, women were just beginning to enter the engineering field in significant numbers. This was a previously male-dominated profession. After a few years working in this industry, I got married and continued my engineering profession while assuming a new role as a homemaker. Now, I had a husband and home to care for in addition to my full-time job. After the birth of my first child, I retired from engineering to become a stay-at-home mom and a homemaker.

I am not saying that women should not go to college or have careers and other interests or ministries. Please don't misunderstand what I am saying. I don't regret a minute of my college and career experiences, and I encourage young women to pursue those avenues. Whether or not you work outside your home, you are still a *homemaker* if you have a husband or children. We need to always remember the high calling we have as wives and mothers to nurture and care for our families. Gladly do it well. *After we first serve and meet the needs of our household, we are free to do anything else God gives us the desire and opportunity to do.*

Little Things Mean So Much

Little things can mean a great deal to your family. Study each member to find out what little things are huge in his or her mind. Different things mean love to each person. It may be something like calling home when you are late so they won't worry. A love note tucked in a suitcase or lunchbox can remind them of your affection when they are away from home. Lots of hugs and kisses may speak volumes of love to your family.

My husband once told his friend that he had never taken a trip away from home without a few homemade cookies tucked in his suitcase. When he got to his hotel room, those cookies reminded him of the love and comforts of home. The funny thing was that I had no idea I had always done this for him. Nor did I realize how much it meant to him. Need I say that the travel-cookie ritual will continue? He's so worth it. I want him to know how important he is.

I love when my husband brings me little presents when he travels. Sometimes it's as simple as the lotion bottle from the hotel or the peanuts from the airplane. It seems so silly, but he knows that I appreciate it. Numerous phone calls to "check on me" also make me feel loved. My husband also knows that a little bag of M&M's candy on Sunday afternoon says a huge "I love you" to me.

My young boys like for me to take them on special adventures; it may be to the zoo, to McDonald's or on a nature walk around the yard. One of our favorite adventures is a game we call "Treasure Hunt". I hide the treasure, usually candy or a small toy, make a treasure map and plant clues to guide them to the treasure. It's not the size of the treasure that excites them, it's the time devoted preparing the hunt for them. They feel special.

As a mother of young boys, I invest hours in racing cars on the floor, playing baseball, soccer, golf, and other original games, building LEGO masterpieces, reading books and playing dinosaurs. They like these things, and so do I. When we love our children and their unique interests, they will feel appreciated and secure. They know when we genuinely care.

Gold Nugget:

Children desperately need to know that their "world", their interests and their concerns are important to their parents.

We all love to receive *sincere appreciation*. A child walked into the kitchen one day and said, "Mom, stop. Let me just look at you." She did. He smiled warmly and replied, "Mom, I just love your smile." As you can imagine, she savored those lovely words for days. She was delighted that her child knew how to express *genuine appreciation.*

Take the time to do the little things. Little things can mean "big love" to the recipients. Give sincere appreciation. Show them you care.

Dinner and Family Time

Many feel that the family gathering around the table at dinnertime is only found on the "Leave It To Beaver" television reruns. Few would argue that the dinner table is a wonderful opportunity to develop a true family identity. Fewer would say they observe this sacred family time regularly.

Many women feel like total failures because they don't have everyone present every night with a home cooked meal consisting of roast beef, mashed potatoes, one green vegetable and freshly baked bread. Just remember, June Cleaver lived in a television studio.

We must examine *what* makes the dinner time ritual so wonderful:

1. All the family members are there ***together without distractions.***

2. They are ***participating in the same activity*** - eating.

3. The family growth occurs by ***focusing on each other, listening, sharing and practicing good conversation and manners.***

It can be a real time of encouragement if parents set the

proper example. *Apply these three criteria to any time you are together and you will have fertile ground for family bonding*.

I am convinced that family unity and peace can be accomplished even with a variety of schedules and lifestyles. Don't beat yourself up if little Jimmy has to eat at four o'clock before soccer practice. You can control your schedule and establish those sacred family times. Dinnertime is ideal, but you must be flexible.

There was a time when our family had our quality family time from eight to ten at night over a bowl of popcorn on the family room floor. We all knew that was our special time to share the day, exchange loving conversation and be physically close. Everyone was present. The goal is to create a sense of unity, intimacy and security within the family unit. The security within your family can be heavily influenced by your attitude and the peace you demonstrate before them. They are watching you.

Love at the Table

Mealtime can be a physical display of love to children. Your effort to provide good nutrition, tasty food and loving conversation can deeply impact your children.

I remember a school assignment in the third grade when we were studying food groups and nutrition. Our assignment was to write down everything we ate for dinner and report it the next day for a nutritional analysis. I told my mom about the assignment and, of course, she prepared a well-balanced feast. I was so proud to tell my teacher I had all the food groups covered and even ate second helpings. Then the teacher asked my friend Marnie what she had for dinner... ice cream and milk. I couldn't believe it! In my eight-year-old mind, I thought, "What kind of mother would feed her growing child ice cream and milk for dinner?" I thanked my mom for loving me more than Marnie's mom loved her.

As a mother now, I must admit I have provided worse meals for my family than ice cream and milk. Providing good food is not the only important part of mealtime. More than just physical food, mealtimes also provide spiritual and emotional food. It's not so much the food that is important, but the loving, accepting environment where it is eaten.

Special effort at mealtime can go a long way with my family. Each member feels so special when we have his favorites. One of my favorite childhood memories was my mom cooking spaghetti (usually on Friday night). It marked the start of a fun weekend. Saturday night was traditionally grilled hamburgers or steaks, baked potatoes and salad. I looked forward to it.

What traditions do you have in your family? Why not start some? But you're not Betty Crocker? Don't worry; buy one basic cookbook and use it. Cooking is as easy as installing mini-blinds. Ask your friends who cook to write down the three recipes their families most enjoy. Try something that doesn't come from a box, bag or can. Your family will be flattered (and maybe surprised).

Use mealtime to celebrate special days or even regular days. You can celebrate obvious holidays or birthdays, but what about celebrating days when "daddy's back in town", "we won the soccer game", or "I learned to count to 20"? Be creative. Some of my favorite ways to make mealtime special include hand-written notes on napkins or paper plates, homemade table decorations, picnic on the family room floor and china in the dining room. My boys also like eating ice cream out of tiny plastic baseball helmets.

Eating out as a family can be a joy too, particularly if your children have mastered behavior in restaurants. The time you would have spent cooking and cleaning up can be spent enjoying your family while someone else does the work for you. Practice showing appreciation for meals out as well as meals prepared at home; adults and children should be gracious by always thanking the hostess.

What Are Children?

> *"You can learn many things from children.*
> *How much patience you have, for instance."*
>
> *- Franklin P. Jones*

Do your kids frustrate you? Do you fail to see the big picture amidst the daily routine? Does being with your children exhaust you? Do you worry about how they will turn out? If so, you are a normal parent. Here's a list of principles that may help ease the journey and make it more meaningful.

1. <u>Children are not perfect</u>.

You are not perfect either, right? So don't be upset that

your kids are not perfect. Only one person has ever been, and He is God's Son. Do not be surprised when children make mistakes, exercise poor judgement or disappoint you.

A first-time parent may be horrified when her precious, angelic twenty-month old lashes out with a boisterous "MINE!" and then bites the arm of an innocent child. What went wrong? Nothing, your child is normal. You must *take action* and *train* her heart in the ways of the Lord. She won't learn what is right or wrong unless you teach her. She needs to know where the boundaries lie and what the consequences of crossing those boundaries are.

2. <u>Children are childish *(Teenagers are teenager-ish)*</u>.

Children are immature and **will do** childish things. They make childish noises, play childish games and have childish emotions. We cannot expect them to have the self-control of an adult at three years or even thirteen years of age. But we can train them and help them gain control as they mature.

3. <u>Children are trusting</u>.

Children are born believing that you will love and care for them. They can also learn not to trust when people show themselves untrustworthy. Work hard to preserve their trust in you.

4. <u>Children have personalities</u>.

Your child's God-given personality may or may not match yours. It is not inferior or superior to yours, just different. It may even drive you crazy at times. A key to a great relationship with your child is taking the time to understand your child's specific personality. You must work hard to understand how to communicate effectively with him. Ask yourself, "What can I do or say to best communicate love to my child?"

If you have more than one child, I bet they have different personalities. Even identical twins often have totally opposite personalities; their mothers can often differentiate their demeanors at birth. Make it your challenge to know your children well.

5. <u>Children are lumps of clay ready to be molded into something beautiful</u>.

Each child is born with amazing potential. God created man differently than the animals. Some animals give birth and abandon their young after a short time; others will lay eggs and never see their offspring hatch. But God had something better for man. God designed the human family to be a strong unit, a place of protection and provision.

Parents are charged to *train* their children as well as provide for their physical needs. Children also are commanded to *obey* their parents. This is the beginning of teaching respect for authority of both God and man. Animals may teach their young how to survive, but man has the privilege and responsibility of teaching his children moral values. If we as parents don't mold our children with God's values, the world will mold them with its ungodly values.

6. <u>Children are blessings.</u>

We know this is true, but some days it is harder to see them as blessings than on other days. If you have children, stop and thank God for entrusting your children to you. Then go and tell them. Say to them, "You are a blessing from God, and I just wanted you to know that I love you. I am blessed to be your mother."

Motherhood is a blessing. On some days it may seem like a burden. God can use the challenges of motherhood to mold your heart and refine your character. Don't let your motherhood frustrate you, but let it purify you into God's holy woman.

Gold Nugget:

Let your motherhood not be a hindrance, but a vehicle to your personal and spiritual growth.

Worldchangers

I like to refer to my boys as little "worldchangers". I define a worldchanger as *one who has the potential to positively change the world with his life*. I don't know the plans God has for them, but I do know that God created them for a special purpose. I like to live with this kind of *expectation* for their lives. I also view my husband as a world-changer. How would you treat your children or husband if you thought of them as worldchangers?

It's fun to imagine what our children might be like when they grow up. We try to focus on the character traits that we want our children to have. Day by day we encourage, instruct, discipline and demonstrate in order to instill the godly qualities we want in their lives. Of course, a primary goal is to see them accept Christ as their Savior and Lord.

Every mother has expectations and aspirations for her children. She wants the best for them. Her words can significantly impact their future. For instance, a child who is told he is worthless and can never amount to anything may believe it and live up to those expectations. And a child who is told God has great things for him to do may just grow up to believe it and do those things. Do you think George Washington's mother viewed him as a worldchanger as she nurtured him and trained him in the ways of God?

I often think about Moses' mother placing her infant in a basket to float in the river. Did she know he was a worldchanger, or did she think he would probably meet the fate of all the other Hebrew boys? I believe she *knew* God had a plan for him. God blessed her faithfulness by letting her nurse young Moses for the Pharaoh's daughter.

Mary, the mother of Jesus, knew from the time of her miraculous conception that Jesus had a special purpose. Can you imagine the pressure of being the mother of God's Son? Talk about stress! (I always wondered if she had morning sickness and heartburn when she was pregnant with Jesus.)

Mary's heart must have been heavy at times as she realized Jesus' ultimate purpose was to die for the sins of the world. She had faith in God's plan as she raised the great

Worldchanger. May we be faithful to the task, like Mary, as we care for our worldchangers.

Teach Your Children to Pray

How do you teach children to pray? It is simple. Pray with them and for them. Children turn on the little tape recorders in their minds everyday to learn how to live. We just have to make sure the right information gets recorded.

> *"And you must think constantly about these commandments I am giving you today. You must teach them to your children and talk about them when you are at home or out for a walk; at bedtime and the first thing in the morning"* (Deuteronomy 6:6-7(TLB)).

When our family prays at mealtimes, we *give thanks*. Really, we thank God for our food, family, guests and any other things we are particularly thankful for at the time. Most of our mealtime prayers contain no supplication, just thanksgiving for the blessings God has given us. We chose not to teach our children a memorized "blessing" to say at the table, because we wanted them to learn that you can tell God anything in your own words when you pray.

When we head out in the car, we pray for God's blessings on the day, for safety and anything else my children want to pray about. Sometimes they don't want to pray about anything; other times they want to pray for someone they know who is sick or needs help. Their requests are so precious. It is exciting to see them understand that a loving, omnipotent God hears their prayers.

At bedtime I pray with each child and thank God for his blessings on his life. I thank Him for peace and rest that night and for strength and health in his body. I pray for God's protection for his body, mind, soul and spirit. I pray for his salvation. I pray for the character traits I see (or want to see) God developing in his life. I may pray the same words every night, but I feel it is important for them to hear my spoken words as I pray for these blessings in their lives. I try to pray words from scripture, since we know God's Word is truth and He is faithful to his word.

I encourage my children to pray to God for forgiveness when they disobey. At ages two and four, the offense committed was probably disobeying Mom or Dad, displaying selfishness or not treating someone with love and respect. After appropriate discipline has been instilled in their bedrooms, I ask them to ask God for forgiveness for their disobedience or unkind act. At a young age children can understand disobeying God's word and the cleansing power of God's forgiveness.

One day my boys had been bored in the backseat of the car too long, so they started getting silly. Their behavior snow-balled until it became very loud and inappropriate for the car. I reminded them that we have a car rule about using indoor voices. I had issued the warning, so the next offense would require disciplinary action. Realizing that "it takes two to tango", one of them silently prayed for God to give him self-control so that the two of them would not disobey. He remained silent the rest of the trip, while the other continued misbehaving. He told me later that he had prayed and that God helped him stay in control.

Prayer is not a privilege exclusively for adults. I don't think God discriminates between the prayers of children and adults. He honors prayers offered in faith. He loves to talk with all who know Him, young and old.

Gold Nugget:

Teach your children to pray by praying with them and for them.

Chapter 10
Dare to Live Bigger

Dream Big

> *"Dreaming big dreams is God's way of helping you do the impossible. Following through on your dreams helps strengthen your belief in a power greater than yourself because you know you couldn't possibly perform such feats alone."*

> *- Wally "Famous" Amos*

Joseph, one of my Bible heroes, was a great dreamer. God gave him a dream in which the sun, moon and stars bowed down to him. From then on he knew he was chosen to be in a position of great authority. However, being the second youngest of twelve sons, it was illogical and unlikely that he would even be in a position over his family, so they laughed at his dream. (Your family may be the first to laugh at your dream, even though they love you.)

Because of their jealousy and hatred, Joseph's brothers sold him as a slave. Then they lied to their father by claiming a wild animal ate him. Little did Joseph know that this "unfortunate" incident was the beginning of his journey to success.

Do you think it was hard for Joseph to see himself in a position of authority while he was a slave, the lowest in social status? God had greater plans for Joseph. He kept believing and doing what he knew was right.

Then Joseph found himself accused, yet innocent, and thrown into prison. How many rulers or leaders start off with prison records? Nevertheless, Joseph believed God's plan and His power to complete it. He held firm, worked hard and pleased both God and men with his integrity. He was experiencing success even though it didn't appear so on the outside. You can read the details of this fascinating story in Genesis 40.

God enabled Joseph to interpret the Pharaoh's dreams to mean that Egypt would have seven years of agricultural plenty followed by seven years of famine. Then Joseph was placed in charge of storing food from the plentiful harvests so the nation could survive during the famine. What an enormous task! But God equipped Joseph as the noble leader to execute the food storage and distribution. Eventually, Joseph became second in command to the Pharaoh of Egypt. He had proven himself as a competent leader of people.

During the famine, Joseph's brothers came to Egypt seeking food. Since many years had passed, the brothers didn't recognize Joseph. What a precious moment it must have been for Joseph to see them again. Being a man of godly character, he forgave them for mistreating him years ago. (I do love how Joseph made his brothers sweat a little bit before he revealed his identity to them.) Joseph was successful; there was no need for revenge.

Because of Joseph's success, Jacob's family and the nation of Israel was saved and blessed. Dream fulfilled! Joseph couldn't see his dream happening along the way, but he believed, persevered and trusted God.

An Acorn in My Belly Button

One of my most influential teachers told my eighth grade science class how he wanted to be buried when he died. He didn't want the traditional coffin and grave where his body would be protected from the earth. He said, "Just dig a hole in the ground, put an acorn in my belly button and cover me up with dirt. In the years to come, an oak tree will grow, and people will see *me* all over it." He meant this literally, not metaphorically.

My teacher wanted to produce something with his life that would live on after he was dead and gone, something that would be significant forever. I'm not sure I want to be plastered all over an oak tree, but I do want the fruit of my labor to last for eternity.

What are you doing today that will proclaim what you have done with your life just like a towering oak tree? Will you be remembered after you are dead and gone? Or will your life end when your grave is sealed? Have you invested

your life in other people? However short or long your life is
here on earth, it is your opportunity to make *your mark.*
Your life can make a difference. The rewards are waiting in
heaven.

Be Fruity

In Matthew 7:17, Jesus said, *"Likewise every good tree
bears good fruit, but a bad tree bears bad fruit."* We are all
like trees bearing fruit: good or bad, plenty or sparse. Our
fruit gives us away; we cannot pretend to be Christians. How
fruity are you?

> *"But the fruit of the Spirit is love, joy, peace,
> patience, kindness, goodness, faithfulness,
> gentleness and self-control. Against such
> things there is no law" (Galatians 5:22-23).*

The Holy Spirit indwells believers and can produce this
fine list of virtues in our lives. He makes it possible to
overcome our sinful nature (Galatians 5:19-21) and display
the fruit of the Spirit. If there is no evidence of the fruit of
the Spirit in your life, you should check the status of your
relationship with God. Do you have a saving relationship
through faith in Christ?

It is impossible to grow a tree that bears fruit without first
planting a seed. When you accept Jesus as your Savior, the
Holy Spirit is like a seed planted in you. This seed won't
produce a weed; it's a Christian seed. Without the Holy
Spirit in your life, it is impossible to bear fruit.

The seed needs to be nurtured with "good stuff" in order

to grow strong and bear fruit. What kind of "good stuff"?
For nourishment it needs the Word of God. It needs to be
watered with the living waters of a fresh relationship with
God. It needs the protection and nurturing of the body of
Christ (fellowship with other believers) to care for it as a
farmer watches over his tender plants. Given time, this seed
will bear good fruit. This fruit may contain many seeds which
when sown will multiply for generations to come.

> *"The one who sows to please his sinful
> nature, from that nature will reap destruction;
> the one who sows to please the Spirit, from
> the Spirit will reap eternal life" (Galatians
> 6:8-9).*

Sow Generously

*You can count the seeds in an apple, but you can't count
the apples in a seed.* One tiny seed may eventually produce a
huge orchard.   Planting "spiritual" seeds in others can
multiply into great numbers of Christians. We can invest in
the lives of other people by planting the seed (the gospel) in
their hearts, watering (teaching) them or nurturing
(encouraging) them.   This is our responsibility and our
privilege.

> *"Remember this: Whoever sows sparingly
> will also reap sparingly, and whoever sows
> generously will also reap generously" (2
> Corinthians 9:6).*

Are you sowing seeds of life? The more you sow, the

more you reap.

Gold Nugget:
Sow big; reap big!

What Are You Becoming?

Do you know deep down in your heart that you were created for a purpose, destined to do something great? You have a glimpse of the greatness that is within you. There is someone you want to become, something you want to do or some ways you want to change for the better. You can visualize it in your mind. You often dream that someday you will just be like "that" or one day you will wake up and have accomplished some great task.

The great accomplishments and great achievers in this world were not produced overnight. The journey to success began long before the success was ever noticed. The seeds of greatness were first buried deep within the soil long before any hint of fruit was ever seen. The seeds contained the vision and the desire to see it fulfilled.

*What seeds of greatness are **within you?*** What do you want to become? What character traits do you want in your life? Which ones do you want to work on first? What do you want your relationships to be like? What responsibilities do you want to maintain? What impact do you want to have on the world? What dreams do you have? **Write them down.** Define specifically what you want or what you want to become. (This may take some time and deep thought and prayer.) These goals should line up with the priorities of your public and private life.

Get Started Becoming

"You don't just 'luck into' things. You build step by step, whether it's friendships or opportunities."

- Barbara Bush

The way you grow the seeds of greatness within you is to **start becoming what you want to become.** Sounds simple. Many people never become what they want simply because they *never start.* Don't make this foolish mistake. After you have a clear picture of what you want to become, GET STARTED.

1. Get Serious

When you are serious about your dreams, you will be willing to sacrifice in order to obtain them. To achieve anything worthwhile, you must be willing to **sacrifice** something in order to gain something greater. For example, to lose weight you may choose to give up ice cream sundaes and put in some time at the gym in order to have a slimmer body.

Most people either have or will attempt to lose weight in their lifetime. For many people weight loss is a constant battle. We often procrastinate, "I'll get serious about it next week after vacation or next year when my life slows down". And then we feel sorry for ourselves when we can't fit into our clothes.

Gold Nugget:

You will never become what you are not now becoming.

We should not expect to see any positive changes in our lives (or bodies) until we *make* some positive changes. To lose weight, you must burn more calories than you consume. A consistent change in your diet and exercise should do it. Positive thinking about losing weight will not slim your hips and thighs; it takes *action*. You must start doing something to succeed.

2. <u>Get Motivated</u>

Motivation helps us start becoming what we want to become. Find your motivation. You may be motivated to become a godly wife by the fear of failing at marriage. You desire a successful, loving marriage. A great marriage doesn't happen by accident or overnight. Your relationship will improve when you *choose* to improve it. It can become as great as you want it to be! Start working on it today. Start working on yourself today.

3. <u>Eliminate De-motivation</u>

The first step to improving you may be to remove all

de-motivation from your speech and your thoughts. Negative thoughts like "I can't" and "I'll never" will de-motivate you. Replace them with "I can" and "I will". You can become what you *want* to become. Be patient, it will happen!

4. Get Encouragement

You will need some source of **encouragement** to achieve your dreams. Surround yourself with people who are like-minded and will cheer you on. Avoid the people around you who will be jealous of your success and achievements; you don't need any dead weight.

5. Get Tough

There will be times when your dreams will seem impossible, and the whole world will be telling you so. This is when you need to **get tough**. You will need a tough skin to endure criticism. You will need a tough attitude to not let failures get the best of you. You will need a tough mind to believe you can succeed when you face failures.

Excellence

> *"Whatever you do, work at it with all your heart, as working for the Lord, not for men..."*
> *(Colossians 3:23).*

We represent the Lord in all we do. We should strive for excellence. The noble woman in Proverbs 31 did, and she earned quite a reputation for her excellence. She was not just excellent in her work, but also in her character and her positive attitude.

> *"Praise her for the many fine things she does.*
> *These good deeds of hers shall bring her*
> *honor and recognition from even the leaders*
> *of the nations" (Proverbs 31:31 (TLB)).*

You may never receive the recognition you deserve from world leaders, but those around you will know you strive for excellence in what you do. More importantly, you can bring honor to the Lord as you let His excellence shine through your life.

My mother is an artist. She sells beautiful watercolor paintings to decorators through galleries. She brought home one of her paintings that had been in a gallery for a while and immediately thought it would look great in my home. When I saw it, I knew it was perfect, too. It was a classic scene from Charleston, South Carolina, which complimented my decor. I was ready to frame it, but she insisted that she "touch it up". She wanted to update a few of the colors, and darken a few areas. I said, "Really, Mom, it is fine just like it is." She replied, "No, a lot of people will see it hanging in your house, and I want it to be my very best." I forgot that the painting reflected my mom's talent and creativity. She didn't want to have anything but the very best on display in her daughter's home.

What a great lesson. Do we strive to do our best? Our "work" is on display before the world and the Lord. Are we proud or ashamed of our work? Is our work excellent? Does it reflect the Lord?

Self-Discipline

Discipline involves bringing yourself under control. A life lived with self-control can be a shining testimony to the world of the power of God. Young women specifically are charged in Titus 2:5 *"to be self-controlled and pure, to be busy at home, to be kind, and to be subject to their husbands, so that no one will malign the word of God."*

We are not supposed to go through life doing, saying, thinking or having anything we want. We must train ourselves to resist our natural desires and to do what is right and godly.

A life without self-control is open to attack and destruction. A warning is found in Proverbs 25:28, *"Like a city whose walls are broken down is a man who lacks self-control."*

Gold Nugget:

Practice self-discipline by denying yourself something everyday.

We discipline our children so they will learn to have control over themselves. The end result is that they will be obedient to God and human authority and be a pleasure to be around. They will be able to control their behavior and respect others. They will have a foundation of discipline and self-control when things don't always "go their way" later in life.

Self-discipline will give you the power and freedom to accomplish extraordinary things in your life. God wants you to have self-discipline and to overcome the weaknesses of your flesh. In 2 Timothy 1:7, we are encouraged *"For God did not give us a spirit of timidity, but a spirit of power, of love and of self-discipline."*

Be Strong and Courageous

One of my favorite Bible stories is Joshua's quest for the Promised Land with the Children of Israel. Joshua was a man who trusted God to help him live *bigger* than he was. It was Joshua's job to lead the children of Israel to the Promised Land where God promised to bless them. This was no glamorous job! The people had wandered in the desert for forty years, their leader (Moses) was dead, and they faced numerous obstacles including the people of Jericho.

> *"Have I not commanded you? Be strong and courageous. Do not be terrified; do not be discouraged, for the Lord your God will be with you wherever you go"* (Joshua 1:9).

This was how God encouraged Joshua before setting out on this quest. Do you think Joshua wondered what troubles were before him that might *terrify* him? There were many.

God told Joshua that He would deliver His people to the Promised Land, and Joshua **believed** it. Joshua was strong and brave. The journey was full of difficulties and dangers, but God did some amazing, miraculous things to encourage the people and protect them. He crumbled a city's walls at the sound of trumpet blasts. He divided the Jordan River so the people could cross on dry land. He made the sun stop in the sky for almost a day. He gave miraculous victory in military tactics throughout the conquest of Canaan. These thrilling stories are found in the book of Joshua. There was no doubt that God was leading Joshua and his people just as He promised.

God didn't promised Joshua an easy journey. Instead He told him, again and again, to be strong and courageous and assured him that he would succeed. Likewise, your journey may not be easy, but you can follow Joshua's example and know that "your God will be with you wherever you go".

Chapter 11
Dare to Succeed Everyday

Don't Be Afraid to Move on

A lady once shared with me that her husband was offered a job promotion that involved moving to a smaller city. I said, "That's great, I bet you are excited." She was not. In fact, she didn't "let" him take the promotion because she didn't want to leave the comfortable life she had established for herself and for her children. She was afraid to move on and leave what was familiar and good for what was unknown and possibly better.

Deep in my heart, I felt like she was making a selfish mistake. Eventually, he took a job with another company which required him to travel every week. He had his life; she and the kids had their lives. I was not surprised when I ran into her a year later and she told me they had separated.

Moving on can be scary, and it can test our faith. The children of Israel were faced with many trials of their faith as they made the journey from slavery to freedom in the Promised Land. Many of them wished they were back in slavery in Egypt rather than being led to possibly die in the desert along the journey. The Lord wanted them to trust Him and obey His commands as they moved on into the unknown. Something better, the Promised Land, awaited them! Sometimes, we've just got to leave our comfort zone and move on to the bigger and better.

Look for Opportunity Ahead

"When one door of happiness closes, another one opens. Often we look so long at the closed door, that we do not see the one that has been opened."

- Helen Keller

A young lady was venting her woes about moving away from her hometown. She said, "I've got everything here - my church, my doctor, my hairdresser..." Her friend assured her, "They have all those things where you are going, too. Besides, you never know, you may find a better church, doctor and hairdresser than you have now!" Be hopeful about the future. Move on.

My husband and I moved and changed situations frequently in our early years of marriage. It was great. We love change. We love new places, new people and new opportunities. Of course, it wasn't always easy. We try to have an optimistic outlook on change - we can't grow without change.

Gold Nugget:
Change is inevitable;
growth is optional.

You Can Do More than You Think You Can

When my first child was born, I was so overwhelmed by the demands of motherhood that I felt like I couldn't get anything done. I called it living in "survival mode". I felt that I had a successful day if I had done nothing more than care for my baby, get the mail and take a shower before my husband got home from work. On days that I accomplished more, such as cleaning the toilets or paying a few bills, I felt like a super woman.

Since then I have learned an amazing truth: *I can do so much more than I think I can.* When we set higher standards for ourselves and have plans to accomplish things, we can do more.

We tend to become so complacent with where we are and resist the challenge to do more, be more or have more of whatever we desire. Instead of excelling, we settle for a life of mediocrity. If we're not moving forward, we are moving backward.

I often think back to the things I was able to accomplish during my college days: working like a dog to get an engineering degree (I'm not very smart, so I had to work really hard), discipling other students involved in a campus ministry, being chaplain of a fraternity's little sisters, maintaining great friendships, having a social life including some dating, running to stay fit and teaching Physics labs. I had fun doing all these things, and I didn't normally feel overwhelmed. It was a fruitful time with *the fastest rate of personal growth in my life.*

I realize the keys to this productive time were:

- Focusing on my objectives in each area

- Budgeting my time

- Saying "no" to activities that would waste my time or didn't support my objectives- (very little television)

- Being <u>motivated</u> to accomplish my objectives

Granted, in college I was totally independent, and my life was far less complicated than it is today. But is there a way I can be just as productive and accomplish just as much today? Yes, by using the same four principles listed above.

You are YOU! God wants you to move on from where YOU are today. Don't look back, you can't change yesterday. Move forward! You can do more than you think you can! I believe in you and the One who made you for a great purpose.

Motivation Makes the Difference

Have you ever noticed how much you can get done the day before you go on vacation? How about the day before company arrives at your home? You suddenly get motivated to vacuum the floor and wash the guestroom sheets. When you move to a new town and get hungry, you are motivated to find a grocery store. If you are properly motivated, you *will take action* and get the important things in life done.

Today, I am motivated by the visions that I want my life, my family and my ministry to be like. I am constantly working toward that vision. This vision motivates me to work hard and be productive. I have physical, social, business, spiritual and family goals. Some of my effort may not be evident for years. For example, one of my objectives is teaching each of my children to have a moral conscience, a healthy self-image and good people skills. This will take years, but every day of effort is accomplishing my objective.

Another foundational goal of my life is to have a peaceful, orderly home that is a place of ministry to my family and guests. This is a daily battle. Some days I make big strides; other days I slide back two steps. I believe this objective is being accomplished over the long term.

Gold Nugget:

I am motivated by my desire to have a home and family pleasing to the Lord.

Are You a "Superwoman"?

We all want to be Superwomen. Every time I feel like I'm doing great, I see another woman who appears to "have it all together". I wonder, "How can she do it all when I can't?"

Comparing ourselves in this way can be either a positive or negative experience. Positively, she can spur us on to be the best we can be. Negatively, we can feel jealous, unworthy and defeated that we can't accomplish more with our lives.

You are a real Superwoman if you are focused on your objectives and motivated to accomplish them. You strive to be your best with a *can-do* attitude and an enthusiasm that spurs others on in their work. You steadily work along doing the right things without hearing the cheer of the crowd. You know from Whom your strength comes. He is your constant joy and strength.

> *"The Lord is my strength and my shield; my heart trusts in him, and I am helped. My heart leaps for joy and I will give thanks to him in song"* (Psalms 28:7).

One More Mailbox

I have enjoyed various forms of exercise most of my life. The two times I needed it most were after the birth of each of my sons. I must admit, I did put on a few extra pounds during each pregnancy. Cookies just seemed to scream my name. After all, you can't drink four glasses of milk a day without a few cookies.

Six weeks postpartum, I was ready to lose that baby blubber. So I began running, if that's what you call huffing and puffing down the driveway. At first the neighbor's mailbox was my goal. Then each day, I would go "one more mailbox" farther.

I continued my "one more mailbox" technique. Bit by bit, anything's a cinch. After a few weeks, I started to see a little progress, and more importantly, I was feeling better about myself. This exercise was stimulating my brain and flooding it with all those neurotransmitters that energize you and help you feel good about yourself. This gave me more energy and a more positive outlook on my life. No more "baby blues"!

My supportive husband was a huge help. I would nurse the baby right before he came home from work. Dinner was ready and waiting on the stove. When he walked through the door, I gave him a quick kiss, handed him the baby and darted out the door for thirty minutes of running. It was a glorious time of quiet and momentary freedom. I knew I didn't want to maintain this type of schedule, but I needed to do it for a short time to get myself back in shape.

My husband then suggested I set a goal to run in a 5K (3 miles) race only six weeks after I began running. I don't like setting goals. How could I set a goal amidst my postpartum chaos? But the pressure of a goal helped me focus and gave me something to chase. I now had a reason to put on my shoes and get out the door. I was motivated.

I accomplished my goal of running the 5K race six weeks after I started running. I felt rather silly with my postpartum body flopping slowly along while these 20-year-old cross-country girls (who had not yet experienced cellulite) whizzed by me. But the important thing was I DID IT - *one more mailbox everyday.*

After the second baby, I did the same thing. I started running after six weeks and ran a 5K six weeks later. I felt so proud to see my husband, my 2 year-old and my 12 week-old baby cheering for me in the rain at the finish line.

My husband taught me a great deal about goal setting and discipline. You see, he was just an average guy who set a goal to run a marathon. He had never been more than a casual runner. After gallons of Gatorade, the agony of sore muscles and many lonely hours on the road before the sun came up, he reached his goal. He's my hero!!!

Any realistic goal can be accomplished with consistent, daily effort. Take it one day at a time, one step at a time, or ... *one mailbox at a time.* You can do it!

Lions and Bears

Do you remember what the young shepherd boy named David told King Saul when he wanted to fight the giant Goliath? He told him how he had killed a lion and a bear that attacked his flock of sheep.

> *"The Lord who delivered me from the paw of the lion and the paw of the bear will deliver me from the hand of this Philistine." Saul said to David, "Go, and the Lord be with you"* (1 Samuel 17:37).

I would call victorious encounters with a lion and a bear pretty amazing. Your average young shepherd boy would probably have sacrificed a few sheep in fear of his own life. David knew the Lord gave him these victories, and He could do it again. David also knew there was a special call on his life. He would eventually become the King of Israel and face even more difficult situations.   His courage and faith were tested over and over.   David trusted in a big God.

Perhaps each challenge David faced tested and built his faith for the next one.   We may not face lions, bears or a Goliath, but we all have some type of *giants* in our lives.

Whenever I was facing something difficult in my life, my dad always told me, *"Remember your lion and bear stories"*. He wanted me to remember how the Lord had brought me through some other difficult times and could give me victory again.   I could trust in that same Lord.   I am so thankful for my faithful, prayerful father.

In the Old Testament we read about the times the Lord provided for and delivered the children of Israel.   God often instructed them to build an altar and offer sacrifices to the Lord.   The altar would then serve to remind them of the Lord's past provision and deliverance.   We should look back through our lives and see our "altars" ... and bear skins ... and lion skins ... and giant shields... and remember the faithfulness of our God.

It's Time to Fight

I am reading through the entire Bible this year for the first time.   It's a unique way to read the Word.   If you have never done this, I highly recommend it.   The Bible I'm using gives a daily selection from the Old Testament, New Testament, Psalms and Proverbs.   Reading the Word this way gives you a big picture view of how the whole Bible fits together.

The Old Testament is particularly fascinating to me.   It's

like a History book, an inspirational story and a great action movie all rolled into one. I am amazed at how many battles are recorded in the Old Testament. Kings would go to battle and annihilate every living thing (often tens of thousands of people) in the whole town and then plunder it. King David fought many of these battles. It seems the Lord used him to wipe out many of the evil people of the day.

As I read all the accounts of David's quests, I noticed something profound. The Lord always told David which city or people to attack. He told him that He would give him the victory; and He did, often in miraculous ways. *But, David always had to* **GO to battle**. The Lord didn't tell him to initiate peace talks and request papers of surrender from his enemies. David had to prepare his troops and then *go to battle.*

> *"All those gathered here will know that it is not by sword or spear that the Lord saves; for the battle is the Lord's and he will give all of you into our hands"* (1 Samuel 17:47).

We too need to "*go to battle*". We face things in our lives that we know the Lord will give us victory over, but He wants us to *attack* them. Maybe He wants to test our faith and make us stronger for the next battle. Maybe He wants us to be a testimony for Him. Maybe He wants us to know what it's like to totally trust Him.

Finish Strong

> *"Think about winning before you go to sleep*

and the moment you wake. Remember: Every day, some ordinary person does something extraordinary. Today, it's your turn."

- Coach Lou Holtz

Many teams have started a season by losing a few games and then have gone on to win a championship. It's not how they started that mattered, but how they finished. They finished strong.

Did you get a slow start? Did you lose the first five games of the season of life? Were you injured while coming down the backstretch? Look ahead to the race left before you. Don't look back to see how far you've come or you may boastfully bask in past accomplishments. Or, more likely, you may be discouraged or disappointed about past failures. It's not what's behind that matters, it's what's ahead. What are you doing today that will make tomorrow better? What success habits are you forming? How will you finish strong?

Gold Nugget:

Dwelling on the failures of your past can only slow you down in the race of life like concrete blocks around a runner's feet.

We've all made mistakes. Some are so shameful only we know about them; others we must wear daily like bumper stickers across our chests. Perhaps we now are branded with a reputation for behaving a certain way.

The good news is *IT DOESN'T MATTER*! Once we have confessed it, turned from it and made any necessary restitution, we can freely *MOVE ON*.

Consider the Apostle Paul. Before he became a Christian, he was Saul, a well-known persecutor of Christians. After his conversion, he flushed his past and moved on to boldly spread Christianity throughout much of the world. That's what the power of Jesus' blood can do in a man's life. He was radically changed; he even got a new name.

Do you think there were any whispers among the other believers when Paul walked into church for the first time after his conversion? They didn't realize that he had met the Savior up close and personal. Jesus had made him a brand new man. Paul didn't let his horrible past hinder his ministry. You see, Paul went on to evangelize much of the world, help establish the early church and write much of the New Testament. Paul was able to rise above it all and finish strong. And you can too!

"I press on toward the goal to win the prize
for which God has called me heavenward in
Christ Jesus" (Philippians 3:14).

Put the past behind you. Press on and finish strong.

Choose Your Attitude

Your attitude is a decision you make moment by moment.

You control it, not your circumstances. When "stuff" happens, your reaction and your attitude are totally up to you. They are not beyond your control. Look to the Holy Spirit to give you power and control over your attitude.

Here's a simple acrostic you can use:

A -   Always give thanks

T -   Treat others with kindness and respect; think before you speak

T -   Take negative thinking captive

I -   Invite positive information and people into your life

T -   Talk about solutions not problems

U -   Uplift people whenever you get a chance

D -   Do more than is expected

E -   Expect great things to happen

S -   Stretch and grow daily

You're a Winner, Not a Quitter

In an effort to encourage our young children not to give up when things are difficult, we taught them a simple little phrase, *"You're a winner, not a quitter."* We use this phrase to encourage them in everything from hitting a baseball to writing the ABC's. When we see them getting frustrated while doing something new or difficult, this phrase reminds them not to give up.

I will never forget when my son Josh was just about to master writing the lowercase and uppercase alphabet. We had set a goal for him and planned a great reward for his months of daily persistence. When I knew he was ready, I gave him a "quiz" with which he could finally prove his mastery of the skill. Toward the end of the quiz, he began to get tired and frustrated and wanted to stop practicing for the day. Two-year old Andrew, realizing that this was the big moment for his brother, came in the room shouting, "Josh, *you're a winner, not a quitter! You can do it!*" That was all the encouragement Josh needed to complete the quiz.

Gold Nugget:

You're a WINNER

not a quitter.